The Candlestick Trading

Unlocking the Patterns That Forecast Market Moves

By
Nathan Venture, D

The Candlestick Trading

Unlocking the Patterns That Forecast Market Moves

Table of Contents

Introduction

In the ever-evolving universe of financial markets, where split-second decisions can make or break fortunes, traders and investors constantly seek tools and techniques to decipher market movements. Among these tools, candlestick patterns stand out as one of the most powerful and time-tested methods for forecasting market behavior. They offer not just a snapshot but a nuanced narrative of market sentiments that can guide trading strategies and risk management practices.

The goal of this book is to demystify candlestick patterns, allowing readers to harness their full potential. This exploration will take you from the foundational aspects of candlesticks to advanced applications and integrations with other technical analysis tools. Whether you're a novice trying to understand the basics or an experienced trader looking to enhance your toolkit, this book is designed to elevate your trading proficiency.

Candlestick patterns, with their rich history dating back to Japanese rice traders in the 18th century, provide a graphical representation of price movements. Their beauty lies in their simplicity and their ability to capture the essence of market psychology within a confined space and timeframe. Candlesticks tell stories of bullish optimism, bearish despair, indecisiveness, and continuity, weaving a complex tapestry that traders can decode to gain insights into future price actions.

The journey begins with a thorough grounding in the basics: understanding what a candlestick chart is, its components, and how it has evolved. We break down each part of the candlestick, from the body to the shadows, to give you a fundamental understanding that will serve as the basis for more complex analyses.

Once comfortable with the basics, you will dive into the fascinating world of candlestick patterns. Single-bar patterns, such as the Doji, Hammer, and Shooting Star, serve as the market's early warning signals. They might indicate potential reversals or the start of new trends, offering essential clues for astute traders.

Multi-bar patterns take the analysis a step further, providing a more comprehensive view of market dynamics. Engulfing patterns, Harami, and Piercing Patterns reveal shifts in market sentiment over multiple periods. These patterns uncover the strategies of market participants, pointing towards potential bullish or bearish continuations or reversals.

As you advance through the chapters, you'll learn to identify critical reversal patterns that can signal market turns. These patterns are crucial for traders looking to capitalize on trend reversals, enabling them to enter and exit positions with precision.

But the world of candlesticks isn't solely confined to reversal patterns. Continuation patterns offer a different dimension, giving traders insights into the sustainability of existing trends. Patterns like Windows (Gaps), Tasuki, and On-Neck provide valuable information about market momentum and potential breakout points.

Complex formations such as the Three White Soldiers and Three Black Crows, and the Rising and Falling Three Methods add another layer of sophistication to candlestick analysis. Recognizing and interpreting these intricate patterns will deepen your understanding and improve your trading acumen.

Candlesticks, when combined with other technical tools, can amplify their predictive power. By integrating candlestick patterns with trend lines, moving averages, and volume analysis, traders can develop a multi-faceted approach to market analysis. This synergy allows for a more holistic view of market conditions, reducing the risk of false signals and enhancing prediction accuracy.

The psychology behind candlestick patterns is another critical aspect we'll explore. Understanding the market sentiments and emotional triggers that drive these patterns provides a richer context for their interpretation. By gaining insight into the collective behavior of market participants, traders can make more informed decisions and anticipate market movements with greater confidence.

No trading strategy is complete without robust risk management practices. Candlestick patterns can play a pivotal role in risk management, aiding in the placement of stop-loss orders and determining position sizes. This book will equip you with strategies to protect your capital and maximize returns, ensuring a disciplined and measured approach to trading.

We also delve into the practical applications of candlestick trading, offering real-world examples and case studies. These insights will illustrate how candlestick patterns can be effectively applied in various market scenarios, enhancing your ability to navigate the complexities of live trading environments.

Developing a comprehensive trading plan that incorporates candlestick strategies is another essential skill that this book aims to impart. From setting clear goals to backtesting strategies for efficacy, you'll learn how to construct a robust framework for your trading activities.

Candlestick patterns are versatile and can be applied across different markets, including equities, forex, commodities, and cryptocurrencies. Each market has its unique characteristics, and this book will guide you on how to adapt candlestick patterns to diverse trading environments, enhancing their applicability and effectiveness.

Finally, mastering technical analysis with candlesticks will enable you to integrate them into a broader technical analysis framework. This comprehensive approach will refine your analytical skills and empower you to make well-informed trading decisions consistently.

The journey through this book promises to be enlightening and empowering. It's designed to take you from the basics to mastery, equipping you with the knowledge and tools needed to excel in the dynamic world of trading. Candlestick patterns offer a window into market psychology, and by mastering them, you can unlock new levels of trading success.

Chapter 1:
Foundations of Candlestick Trading

To truly grasp the essence of candlestick trading, it's essential to lay down a solid foundation. This chapter serves as your gateway to understanding the visual and analytical power of candlestick charts, a pivotal tool for deciphering market movements. Originating centuries ago from Japanese rice traders, candlesticks have evolved into a universal language for traders, capturing the intricate dance of market psychology. By breaking down the basic components, including the body and wicks, and exploring their historical roots, we set the stage for mastering the art and science of candlestick patterns. This foundational knowledge is crucial whether you're delving into single candlestick formations or more complex multi-bar patterns in later chapters. Through our journey, we'll blend historical insights with practical applications, ensuring you not only recognize patterns but also harness them to forecast market trends with confidence.

Understanding Candlestick Charts

To truly become adept at candlestick trading, understanding candlestick charts is pivotal. These charts provide a visual representation of price movements, encapsulating the open, high, low, and close for a specific time period. Unlike traditional bar charts, candlestick charts offer more nuanced insights into market sentiment and price action. The body of each candlestick signals the strength of the buyers (bullish) or sellers (bearish), while the wicks offer clues about the market's volatility and potential turning points. Mastering the interpretation of these charts empowers traders to make informed decisions, identify emerging trends, and predict future price movements with greater confidence. As you dive deeper into the world of candlestick charts, you'll find that each candlestick tells a unique story about the market's underlying psychology, helping you to craft well-informed and strategic trading plans.

The History and Evolution of Candlesticks

This is a testament to the profound antiquity and enduring relevance of this mesmerizing form of charting. The origins of candlestick charts date back to the 18th century in Japan, where rice traders first conceived them. These traders, keen on optimizing their profits in the volatile rice markets, developed an innovative way to track price movements. Little did they know, their creations would lay the groundwork for a fundamental tool in modern technical analysis.

The story begins with Munehisa Homma, a Japanese rice trader from Sakata, who is often heralded as the father of the candlestick chart. Homma meticulously recorded the price, volume, and daily market conditions of rice trades, seeking patterns that could reveal the market's direction. Through his diligent analysis, Homma recognized that the market was significantly influenced by emotions like fear and greed. This understanding led him to develop the first candlestick charts, which visually encapsulated these sentiments and market behaviors.

These early candlesticks evolved alongside the rice markets, providing Homma and other traders with a means to anticipate price movements. Unlike the contemporary bar charts used in the West, which only plotted closing prices, candlesticks offered a fuller picture by representing open, high, low, and close prices within a single session. This method allowed for a more nuanced reading of market sentiment. Over time, candlestick charts became an indispensable tool for Homma, who reputedly amassed a considerable fortune utilizing his analytical methods.

Despite their initial success, candlestick charts remained relatively obscure outside of Japan for several centuries. It wasn't until the late 20th century that candlesticks made their journey to the West, thanks in large part to the efforts of technical analyst Steve Nison. In the early 1990s, Nison introduced Western traders to the rich history and practical utility of candlestick charts through his seminal works. His books demystified these once enigmatic patterns, bridging the cultural gap and facilitating their widespread adoption across global financial markets.

The integration of candlestick charts into Western financial analysis marked the beginning of a new era in technical trading. Traders and analysts were quick to recognize the advantages of candlesticks—their ability to convey complex price actions and market psychology at a glance was revolutionary. Combining traditional Western technical tools with Japanese candlestick techniques resulted in more robust and insightful market analyses.

Over the past few decades, the evolution of candlestick charts has been nothing short of extraordinary. Advances in technology and the proliferation of online trading platforms have made these charts accessible to traders at all levels, from institutional investors to individual hobbyists. The visual nature of candlesticks resonates well with the human penchant for pattern recognition, enabling traders to quickly identify potential trading opportunities.

Furthermore, the development of new software tools and algorithms has empowered traders to backtest candlestick patterns, assessing their historical performance across various markets. This empirical approach has not only validated many traditional patterns but has also led to the discovery of new ones. Traders continue to merge candlestick analysis with other technical tools, such as moving averages, trend lines, and volume indicators, to build sophisticated trading strategies that cater to a wide range of market conditions.

The global financial landscape is continually evolving, driven by advancements in technology, changes in market structure, and shifts in investor behavior. Despite these changes, the fundamentals of candlestick charting remain relevant. The core principles developed by early Japanese traders endure, reminding us that human emotions—fear, greed, uncertainty—consistently influence market dynamics. Candlesticks uniquely capture these emotions, offering traders timeless insights into market behavior.

In conclusion, the history and evolution of candlesticks is a fascinating journey that underscores their significance in technical analysis. From the rice markets of 18th-century Japan to the trading floors of modern stock exchanges, candlesticks have proven to be an invaluable tool for understanding market sentiment and predicting price movements. As we continue to innovate and adopt new technologies, the foundational concepts of candlestick charting will undoubtedly remain a cornerstone of successful trading strategies. So, carry forth the wisdom of the past, and let the candlesticks illuminate the way to your future trading endeavors.

Basic Components of a Candlestick

It is critical to understanding and accurately interpreting candlestick charts. Without a solid grasp of these fundamental elements, the nuanced language of candlestick patterns would be lost, rendering any analysis ineffective. So, let's dive right into these components, which form the backbone of our foray into candlestick trading.

At its core, a candlestick is composed of four main elements: the open, high, low, and close prices within a particular time frame. The body of the candlestick represents the range between the opening and closing prices. If the closing price is higher than the opening price, the body is usually white or green, indicating bullish or upward movement. Conversely, if the closing price is lower than the opening price, the body is often black or red, signaling bearish or downward movement.

The lines extending from the top and bottom of the body, commonly known as wicks or shadows, depict the high and low prices during the period. The upper shadow extends from the top of the body to the high price, while the lower shadow runs from the bottom of the body to the low price. These shadows offer insights into market volatility and the price action's range within the chosen time frame.

Don't let the simplicity of these elements fool you. Although the open, high, low, and close data points may seem straightforward, they collectively reveal a significant amount of information about market sentiment and potential future movements. The body, in particular, is crucial because it shows the tug-of-war between buyers and sellers during the specified period. A long body suggests strong buying or selling pressure, while a short body indicates indecision or a lackluster market.

Another crucial aspect is the placement and length of the shadows. A long upper shadow with a short lower shadow may suggest that buyers tried to push the price higher but couldn't sustain the effort, often resulting in a bearish signal. Conversely, a long lower shadow with a short upper shadow can indicate that sellers tried to drive the price down, but buyers regained control, often forming a bullish signal. These nuances can be pivotal for those looking to anticipate market movements accurately.

One common type of candlestick is the Doji, which forms when the open and close prices are almost identical. This pattern is typically regarded as a sign of market indecision and can be a precursor to a shift in market direction. Another is the Hammer, which has a small body at the top with a long lower shadow, indicating that an initial decline was met with strong buying interest. Conversely, the Shooting Star has a small body at the bottom with a long upper shadow, suggesting that an initial rally was overtaken by selling pressure.

Not all candlesticks are created equal in terms of what they tell us about the market. The time frame you choose to analyze can profoundly impact your interpretation. For example, a candlestick representing a month may tell a different story compared to one representing an hour or a minute. Hence, understanding the context within which these candlesticks appear is just as vital as understanding their basic components.

Moreover, the relationship between consecutive candlesticks can form patterns that offer even more predictive power. While single candlesticks can provide valuable insights, multi-bar patterns can provide a more comprehensive view of market sentiment. Recognizing these patterns helps you make more informed trading decisions, thereby enhancing your ability to forecast market turns and trends.

Additional elements occasionally incorporated into candlestick analysis are color variations and enriched visual details to easily distinguish bullish from bearish trends. Advanced charting tools sometimes use different shades or specific patterns within the bodies to indicate varying degrees of buying or selling pressure. While these enhancements can be helpful, they don't stray from the fundamental properties of open, close, high, and low prices.

Understanding these core elements won't just help you read the market; it will also empower you to devise strategies grounded in real data rather than conjecture. Whether you're a day trader looking for quick gains or an investor aiming for long-term returns, mastering these basics is your first step toward more informed and hopefully more profitable trading.

In essence, every candlestick tells a story about market activity within a specified period, reflecting the collective actions of buyers and sellers. The key is learning to read these stories accurately, which starts by understanding and recognizing the basic components of a candlestick. By doing so, you lay a solid foundation for more advanced technical analysis and candlestick interpretation.

With this understanding, you're better equipped to delve deeper into candlestick patterns, explore multi-bar setups, and combine various technical tools for a holistic trading strategy. As we proceed, keep these foundational elements in mind. They will be the lens through which you interpret more complex patterns and advanced chart analysis.

Chapter 2:
Decoding Candlestick Patterns

Transitioning from the foundational knowledge of candlestick charts, the next step in mastering candlestick trading lies in decoding the diverse array of candlestick patterns. Recognizing these patterns equips traders with the ability to predict market movements with greater accuracy. Single candlestick patterns like the Doji, Hammer, and Shooting Star offer insights into potential market reversals or continuations. Building on this, multi-bar patterns such as Engulfing, Harami, and Piercing Patterns provide a richer context, unfolding the intricate dynamics between buyers and sellers. This chapter delves into these patterns' subtleties, enhancing your toolkit for navigating the volatile waters of financial markets. Each pattern not only tells a story of past interactions but also sets the stage for anticipating future price actions, empowering you to make informed, strategic decisions.

Single Candlestick Patterns

Single candlestick patterns may seem deceptively simple, but they hold significant power in the world of technical analysis. These patterns consist of individual candlesticks that provide valuable insights into market sentiment and potential future movements. Key single candlestick formations, such as the Doji, Hammer, and Shooting Star, can act as early indicators of bullish or bearish reversals. Understanding the psychology behind these patterns enables traders to make more informed decisions, improving their ability to anticipate market movements. Through practice and keen observation, one can master the art of interpreting these concise yet potent signals, adding a crucial tool to their trading arsenal.

The Significance of Doji, Hammer, and Shooting Star

These serve as a cornerstone for understanding single candlestick patterns, essential for any trader looking to grasp the market's psychology and improve their technical analysis skills. These three formations are not just isolated indicators but part of a larger tapestry that reveals the sentiments and potential reversals within the market. Knowing when these patterns appear and what they signify can give traders a considerable edge.

The Doji is perhaps one of the most versatile and revealing single candlestick patterns. Its name, which means "mistake" or "blunder" in Japanese, hints at its core nature—indecision. A Doji occurs when the opening and closing prices are virtually identical, resulting in a small or non-existent body flanked by long wicks on either side. This formation vividly captures a battle between buyers and sellers, neither of which gain control. The pattern signals that the current trend may be losing momentum, prompting traders to consider potential reversals or periods of consolidation. Recognizing a Doji in the right market context can be an alert to tighten stops or re-evaluate positions.

In contrast, the Hammer is a bullish reversal pattern that appears after a downtrend and is characterized by a small body at the top of the candle, coupled with a long lower wick. The long wick suggests that sellers drove the price down significantly, but by the end of the trading period, buyers had regained control, pushing the price back up. This shift can be a strong indication that buyers are stepping in and that the previous downtrend may be about to reverse. Hammers can occur in different colors, but the key element is the lower shadow being at least twice the length of the real body, evidencing the day's trading dynamics. Traders should look for confirmation before taking a position, often in the form of a subsequent bullish candlestick.

Then we have the Shooting Star, essentially a bearish counterpart to the Hammer. It is a bearish reversal pattern that appears after an uptrend. The Shooting Star has a small body near its low, with a long upper wick. This shape indicates that buyers were initially in control, pushing the price significantly higher. However, by the end of the trading period, sellers took over, driving the price back down near its opening level. This shift can be a powerful signal that the uptrend may be about to end, making the Shooting Star a critical pattern for identifying potential selling opportunities. Just like the Hammer, traders often seek confirmation from a subsequent bearish candlestick before acting on this pattern.

Understanding the significance of these patterns goes beyond mere identification. Each of these candlestick formations represents a story told through price action. For the Doji, the narrative is one of uncertainty and equilibrium, making it a crucial watchpoint for potential shifts in market direction. When a Doji appears, the market's story is one of balance but also ripe for change, acting as a precursor to a potential shift in trend.

The Hammer's significance is deeply rooted in its appearance during downtrends. Its story is one of resilience and potential turnaround, embodying the struggle and eventual victory of the buyers over the sellers. When you spot a Hammer, it's more than just a pattern; it's a message from the market that the selling pressure may be exhausting, and a bullish reversal could be on the horizon.

Conversely, the Shooting Star serves as a cautionary tale that an uptrend might be nearing its end. This pattern's significance lies in its abrupt shift from bullish to bearish sentiment within a single trading period. When a Shooting Star emerges, it often warns traders that the buyers' euphoria is waning, and selling pressure is mounting. Thus, understanding the Shooting Star helps traders anticipate potential downtrends.

For day traders, recognizing these patterns in real-time can significantly affect trading outcomes. The ability to spot a Hammer at the end of a prolonged downtrend, for instance, might present an invaluable buying opportunity. Conversely, identifying a Shooting Star at the peak of an uptrend might allow a savvy trader to lock in profits before the market turns.

Technical analysts benefit tremendously from these patterns as they function as diagnostic tools for evaluating market health and potential reversals. By incorporating Doji, Hammer, and Shooting Star analyses into broader technical strategies, analysts can add layers of confirmation to their forecasts, resulting in more robust and reliable market assessments.

For investors, particularly those focused on longer-term trends, these patterns can signal opportune moments to enter or exit positions. While individual pattern occurrences may not directly lead to long-term investments, they can serve as alerts to reevaluate holdings and align strategies with the broader market sentiment.

Even finance students and novice traders will find these patterns incredibly educational. By studying Doji, Hammer, and Shooting Star formations, students can gain insight into the emotional and psychological factors driving market movements. This foundational knowledge equips them to better understand more complex patterns and strategies as they advance in their trading careers.

Experienced financial professionals might utilize these patterns as part of a more comprehensive strategy involving other technical indicators, like moving averages or relative strength index (RSI). Integrating these single candlestick patterns with other technical tools can enhance the precision of market entries and exits, providing a more rounded approach to trading.

For self-directed investors and trading enthusiasts, mastering these patterns adds a weapon to their trading arsenal. Recognizing a Doji, Hammer, or Shooting Star at the right moment allows for more informed decision-making, optimizing strategies and potentially increasing returns. They help traders avoid pitfalls of emotional trading by grounding decisions in solid, observable patterns.

From a risk management perspective, these patterns offer essential clues for setting stop-loss orders and determining position sizes. A Hammer indicating a potential bullish reversal might suggest a tighter stop-loss placement to protect against lingering bearish sentiment. Conversely, a Shooting Star might encourage widening stop-losses to secure profits ahead of a possible downturn.

The motivational aspect of understanding these patterns can't be overlooked. Grasping the significance of Doji, Hammer, and Shooting Star can build a trader's confidence and competence. Knowing that each candlestick tells a story allows traders to feel more connected to market movements, transforming abstract price data into actionable insights.

When applying these patterns to real-world trading, it's crucial to incorporate context. Not every Doji, Hammer, or Shooting Star carries the same weight. The market conditions, volume, and preceding trend play significant roles in determining the reliability and impact of these patterns. It's this nuanced understanding that separates skilled traders from novices. Any pattern should be considered within the broader scope of market analysis, reinforcing the idea that trading is as much an art as it is a science.

Incorporating these insights into a daily trading routine can reinforce discipline and enhance decision-making. By routinely scanning for Doji, Hammer, and Shooting Star patterns, traders develop a keen eye for market shifts, allowing for timely action. Over time, this practice can become second nature, empowering traders to navigate the markets with more agility and foresight.

Ultimately, the significance of Doji, Hammer, and Shooting Star patterns lies in their ability to convey market sentiment through visual cues. Mastering

Multi-Bar Candlestick Patterns

In the fascinating world of candlestick analysis, multi-bar candlestick patterns form the bedrock for more nuanced market forecasts. These patterns, including the venerable Engulfing, subtle Harami, and reliable Piercing patterns, offer day traders and technical analysts crucial insights into market sentiment over multiple trading sessions. By understanding the intricacies of these patterns, investors can not only enhance their ability to predict potential reversals but also improve their skill in identifying continuation signals. This deeper comprehension empowers traders to craft more sophisticated and effective trading strategies, blending these patterns with other analytical tools to maximize returns while managing risk wisely. Multi-bar patterns, with their layered complexity, serve as a vital reminder that the financial markets often tell their most compelling stories over multiple chapters, not just single events.

Engulfing, Harami, and Piercing Patterns

These are cornerstones in the world of multi-bar candlestick patterns, deeply rich in information and significance. These patterns mark potential points of market reversals, assisting traders in making informed decisions driven by pattern recognition and statistical probabilities. Understanding these patterns requires mastering the subtle dynamics of market sentiment encapsulated in the interplay of bullish and bearish forces.

Let's start with **engulfing patterns**. An engulfing pattern forms over two candles and signifies a potential reversal in trend. In a bullish engulfing pattern, the second candle completely "engulfs" the body of the first candle, indicating a potential shift from bearish to bullish sentiment. Conversely, in a bearish engulfing pattern, a large bearish candle engulfs a preceding smaller bullish candle, suggesting impending downtrend momentum. Traders often see these patterns as strong signals because the engulfing action demonstrates a decisive shift in market control.

The key to interpreting engulfing patterns lies not only in the size and shape of the candles but also in their contextual placement within existing trends. A bullish engulfing pattern at the end of a downtrend can mark the beginning of a new uptrend, whereas a bearish engulfing pattern at the top of an uptrend can hint at an impending market decline. This is why engulfing patterns are often hailed as reliable indicators for reversals. However, context is crucial; one must look at volume indicators and other technical tools for corroboration.

Next, let's dive into **harami patterns**. The term "harami" comes from the Japanese word for "pregnant," which aptly describes the pattern's appearance. In a harami pattern, a small candle forms within the body of a preceding larger candle. This happens over two days, with the second candle being the "baby" or contained entirely within the "mother" or first candle. A bullish harami occurs during a downtrend, indicating potential upward movement, while a bearish harami appears in an uptrend, signaling a possible downturn.

Harami patterns, though not as dramatic as engulfing patterns, are still valuable. They often represent a pause in the prevailing trend and can signal indecision or a potential reversal. This pause allows traders to gauge whether the market is losing momentum. For instance, a bullish harami in a downtrend suggests that selling pressure might be waning, offering a hint that bulls may step in. Similarly, a bearish harami in an uptrend hints at weakening buying pressure and the potential for bears to gain control.

Finally, we encounter the **piercing pattern**, a powerful bullish reversal signal found at the end of a downtrend. The piercing pattern consists of two candles: the first being a long bearish candle, followed by a long bullish candle that opens below the previous day's low but closes more than halfway into the prior bearish candle's body. This pattern demonstrates a strong change in market sentiment, indicating bullish momentum.

While the setup for a piercing pattern is specific, its implication is straightforward: buyers are beginning to overwhelm sellers. The market opens lower, continuing the downtrend, but strong buying pressure pushes the price up significantly, closing within the previous day's range. This action suggests that bulls are not just preventing further decline but are actively reversing the trend direction.

Recognizing these patterns is integral for several reasons. First, they offer visual cues that help traders anticipate market movements more effectively. Second, they represent the collective psychology of market participants, giving traders insight into underlying sentiment shifts. While these patterns are relatively straightforward to identify, their effectiveness multiplies when combined with other technical analysis tools and a clear trading strategy.

In practice, it's crucial to confirm these patterns with additional indicators. For example, a volume increase during the formation of an engulfing or piercing pattern can significantly bolster the pattern's credibility. Similarly, aligning these candlestick patterns with Fibonacci retracement levels or support and resistance lines can provide a more comprehensive market perspective.

To integrate this knowledge seamlessly into your trading routine, focus on watching out for these patterns in conjunction with your broader analysis. Start by identifying potential setups on daily charts to understand the overarching trends and then zoom into shorter time frames for precise entry and exit points. Training your eye to spot these patterns through consistent practice will gradually build your trading acumen.

It's also essential to appreciate that candlestick patterns like engulfing, harami, and piercing aren't foolproof. False signals can and do occur, which is why risk management strategies, such as stop-loss orders, are vital. Advanced traders often backtest these patterns extensively to understand their success rates over historical data, enabling them to fine-tune their strategies further.

Notably, mastering these patterns goes beyond the technical aspects; it's about developing a robust trading philosophy grounded on patience and precision. As you hone your skills, you'll gain the ability to read between the lines of candlestick patterns, discerning the nuanced interplay of market forces.

In conclusion, **Engulfing, Harami, and Piercing Patterns** are pivotal tools in a trader's arsenal for recognizing potential market reversals. By understanding their formation, context, and implications, you'll be better equipped to foresee market shifts and craft well-informed trading strategies. Coupling these patterns with additional technical analysis reinforces your ability to navigate the complexities of financial markets confidently. But remember, while these patterns provide invaluable insights, the ultimate success in trading hinges on a blend of analytical prowess, strategic planning, and disciplined risk management.

Chapter 3:
Reversal Patterns That
Forecast Market Turns

Reversal patterns are like the market's way of whispering secrets to the astute trader, signaling when a trend is about to take a dramatic turn. These patterns can appear at both market tops and bottoms, serving as early indicators of potential bullish or bearish reversals. For investors, mastering these patterns is crucial; they enable you to anticipate shifts and make informed decisions rather than reacting impulsively. Recognizing formations such as the Double Bottom, Head and Shoulders, and Morning Star can provide you with a tactical advantage. Equipped with this knowledge, you'll be better prepared to capitalize on emerging opportunities while safeguarding your investments from sudden market downturns. So, let's dive into these reversal patterns and turn that whisper into a clear, actionable signal.

Identifying Bullish Reversal Patterns

In the realm of candlestick trading, bullish reversal patterns are a beacon of potential profit. These patterns signal a possible shift in market sentiment, indicating that a downtrend may be nearing its end and an uptrend could be on the horizon. Recognizing these patterns not only enhances your market forecasting skills but also amplifies your trading arsenal, enabling you to seize timely opportunities.

Bullish reversal patterns encompass a variety of formations, each with its unique story about market psychology. Understanding these formations is akin to learning a new language, a language that speaks volumes about the interplay between buyers and sellers. Observe the subtleties in the patterns, for they often reflect a climactic battle where bears (sellers) start to lose their grip, and bulls (buyers) begin to take charge.

Let's start with one of the most well-known bullish patterns: the Hammer. The Hammer represents those moments when the market is testing its lows before reversing upwards. This pattern appears as a short body at the upper end of the trading range with a long lower shadow, suggesting that sellers pushed prices lower, but buyers were strong enough to drive them back up. When the Hammer surfaces at the bottom of a downtrend, it implies that a bullish reversal is potentially underway.

Another key pattern is the Bullish Engulfing. This two-candle pattern involves a small bearish candle followed by a larger bullish candle that entirely engulfs the prior candle's body. This shift in control indicates that the bulls have overpowered the bears, and it's often seen as a strong signal of an impending uptrend. Pay attention to the volume accompanying this pattern; higher volume tends to validate the reversal signal, giving it more weight.

Then there's the Morning Star, a powerful three-candle pattern. It starts with a long bearish candle, followed by a small indecisive candle (which can be either bullish or bearish), and concludes with a long bullish candle. This pattern illustrates the transition from selling pressure to buying interest and often leads to robust bullish moves. The Morning Star not only signifies the end of a downtrend but also the initiation of a new bullish phase, leading to potentially lucrative trading opportunities.

Moving deeper into multi-bar patterns, consider the Piercing Pattern. This consists of a long bearish candle followed by a bullish candle that opens below the previous close and closes above the midpoint of the bearish candle. This formation reveals the resilience of buyers and signals that the selling momentum is waning. Traders often regard the Piercing Pattern as a reliable early indicator of bullish market sentiment.

Recognizing these patterns in the context of market conditions and other technical signals is paramount. You'll want to avoid tunnel vision—don't just focus on the candlestick patterns in isolation. Complement your analysis with other tools like trend lines, moving averages, and volume indicators to get a holistic view of the market. Such comprehensive analysis bolsters your trading decisions and minimizes risk.

Let's take an example to illustrate the power of these patterns. During a historical downtrend in a popular tech stock, a Hammer appeared on the daily chart, which was then confirmed by a subsequent Bullish Engulfing pattern. Coupled with increasing volume and a break above the 200-day moving average, these signals paved the way for a sharp bullish reversal, resulting in significant gains for traders who caught this move.

As you cultivate the skill of identifying bullish reversal patterns, remember that practice is your best ally. Spend time reviewing charts, backtesting your hypotheses, and familiarizing yourself with how these patterns play out in different market contexts. The more you practice, the more instinctual your pattern recognition will become, allowing you to react swiftly and confidently when these signals present themselves.

That said, trading isn't devoid of emotion and psychology. Bullish reversal patterns often follow periods of fear, uncertainty, and heightened selling pressure. As a trader, maintaining a disciplined mindset and adhering to your trading plan is as crucial as recognizing the patterns themselves. Harness emotions for insight but never let them cloud your judgment.

In summary, mastering bullish reversal patterns equips you with the foresight to anticipate market turns and capitalize on new trends. Through diligent study and practice, these patterns become more than just charts; they transform into narratives of market behavior, guiding your trading strategy and enhancing your decision-making arsenal.

Identifying Bearish Reversal Patterns

Understanding and identifying bearish reversal patterns is an invaluable skill for any trader. These patterns signal potential market tops and foreshadow downward price movements, which can inform decisions on holding, selling, or shorting assets. Being adept at recognizing these patterns allows traders to capitalize on market trends and minimize losses, enhancing their overall trading performance.

Evening Star is one of the most powerful bearish reversal patterns. It's a three-candle formation that typically occurs at the end of an uptrend. The first candle is a long bullish candle, followed by a small-bodied candle that gaps up, and finally, a long bearish candle that closes well into the body of the first bullish candle. The evening star indicates buyer exhaustion and the emergence of sellers, signaling a potential market top. Traders should monitor the volume of the third candle for confirmation; a spike in volume heightens the pattern's reliability.

The **Bearish Engulfing** pattern is another classic reversal sign. This two-candlestick pattern consists of a small bullish candle followed by a larger bearish candle that completely engulfs the first one. It suggests that sellers have taken control from the buyers, and it often precedes significant price declines. The size of the candles and the volume accompanying the engulfing candle can enhance the pattern's predictive power. A large bearish engulfing candle on high volume can act as a strong signal for traders to consider closing long positions or initiating short positions.

Sometimes, traders might encounter a **Dark Cloud Cover** pattern, which is also a potent bearish signal. This two-bar formation starts with a strong bullish candle, followed by a bearish candle that opens above the prior high but closes below its midpoint. It indicates a significant shift in market sentiment from bullish to bearish. The deeper the second candle penetrates the first one, the stronger the signal. Volume analysis can further confirm the pattern's validity. Observing a high volume on the second candlestick can provide additional confidence that a downward movement is imminent.

The **Shooting Star** is a straightforward yet highly effective single-candle bearish reversal pattern. Appearing after an uptrend, the shooting star has a small body and a long upper shadow, with little to no lower shadow. This structure reveals that buyers tried to push prices higher but failed, ultimately allowing sellers to regain control. The higher the upper shadow, the more significant the reversal signal, especially if it forms near a key resistance level. This pattern often prompts traders to tighten stop-loss orders on long positions or to consider initiating short positions.

Three Black Crows is a more complex bearish reversal signal involving three consecutive long bearish candles following an upward trend. Each candle typically opens within the previous candle's real body and closes near its low, showing steady selling pressure. This pattern underscores a strong and sustained shift from bullish to bearish sentiment. While the presence of this pattern can be compelling on its own, traders often look for confirmation via volume or additional technical indicators such as moving averages or RSI crossing down from overbought territory.

Traders should also be aware of the **Bearish Harami** pattern. This two-candle formation starts with a long bullish candle followed by a smaller bearish or bullish candle contained within the previous candle's real body. The bearish harami suggests a pause in upward momentum and potential onset of bearish sentiment. It's particularly telling when it forms after a strong uptrend, signaling trader caution. Furthermore, traders can seek additional confirmation through other indicators such as MACD or stochastics that might indicate overbought conditions.

While these patterns can be powerful, it's crucial to couple them with other analytical tools for improved reliability. For instance, combining these bearish patterns with *moving averages* can help traders identify when the broader trend is still downwards, adding more credence to the reversal signal. Similarly, using trend lines can offer additional context, helping to affirm the suspected reversal at major trend lines resistance points.

Volume plays a critical role in verifying any bearish reversal pattern. A significant rise in volume accompanying the formation of a bearish pattern indicates greater participation among traders, bolstering the credibility of the impending reversal. Conversely, low volume may signal that the pattern could be a false alarm. As such, savvy traders often wait for volume confirmation before making trading decisions based on bearish candlestick patterns.

It's also important to comprehend the psychological underpinnings of these patterns. For instance, patterns like the Bearish Engulfing or Dark Cloud Cover reveal sudden shifts in market psychology where buyers begin to lose confidence, and sellers start to dominate. Understanding these psychological shifts helps traders gauge the market's sentiment more accurately and anticipate future price movements more effectively.

Risk management cannot be understated when trading based on bearish reversal patterns. Using tight stop-loss orders just above the high of the pattern formation can help in mitigating potential losses. This strategy ensures that if the market unexpectedly turns bullish, your losses are limited. Position sizing aligned with the risk you're willing to take can also help preserve your trading capital over the long run.

Combining traditional analysis with modern tools like algorithmic scanners can enhance the identification of these patterns. Many trading platforms offer tailored algorithms that can scan various markets for bearish reversal patterns, providing real-time alerts and saving valuable time. Being technologically savvy and leveraging these tools can significantly improve your trading strategy's accuracy.

Ultimately, mastering the art of identifying bearish reversal patterns is an ongoing process of study, practice, and refinement. Each trader may develop their unique approach to recognizing and reacting to these signals. Regular backtesting and keeping a meticulous trading journal can aid in honed strategies and adapt them based on market feedback.

By integrating bearish reversal patterns into a broader trading plan, traders can make more informed decisions. Combining these patterns with other technical indicators and maintaining disciplined risk management strategies can significantly enhance trading outcomes. The more adept you become at identifying these patterns, the better equipped you'll be to forecast market turns and navigate the complexities of financial markets successfully.

Chapter 4:
Continuation Patterns and
Their Predictive Power

As we delve deeper into the world of candlestick trading, it's crucial to explore continuation patterns and their predictive power. Continuation patterns signify that the prevailing trend is likely to persist, which can be an invaluable insight for traders looking to ride the wave of market momentum. These patterns provide a robust framework for anticipating price movements, offering a strategic edge whether the market is trending up or down. For instance, identifying windows (gaps) can reveal market sentiment and potential support or resistance levels. Similarly, patterns like the Tasuki and On-Neck are pivotal in solidifying your understanding of ongoing trends. Mastering these concepts empowers you to project future market behavior with greater accuracy, effectively setting the stage for more informed and precise trading decisions. So, by harnessing the predictive power of continuation patterns, traders can navigate the markets with enhanced confidence and strategic foresight.

Windows (Gaps) and Their Implications

In the world of candlestick charts, gaps, or "windows" as they are often referred to in Japanese candlestick terminology, hold a unique place of importance. These windows are a significant visual cue in chart analysis, representing a price range where no trading occurs. The implication? A gap indicates sudden shifts in market psychology, often fueled by news events, earnings reports, or significant geopolitical developments.

Firstly, it's crucial to understand there are different types of gaps: Common gaps, Breakaway gaps, Runaway gaps, and Exhaustion gaps. Each type has its own unique set of implications and can serve as powerful indicators when you know how to read them. For example, breakaway gaps typically appear at the beginning of a new trend, suggesting a strong move with plenty of market conviction. In contrast, exhaustion gaps occur at the end of a trend, signaling a potential reversal imminent.

Breakaway gaps are particularly noteworthy in the context of continuation patterns, as they often confirm the beginning of a new phase in the ongoing trend. When a stock breaks out of a trading range with a gap, it generally indicates that the market has moved decisively beyond a key level of support or resistance. This type of gap is often accompanied by high volume, lending additional credibility to the movement. For traders, identifying breakaway gaps can provide an opportunity to enter a position early in a new trend, maximizing potential gains.

Conversely, runaway (or measuring) gaps usually occur within an existing trend, indicating a continuation of the prevailing market sentiment. Often, these gaps happen halfway through the move, providing a relative measure of how far the trend might still run. Traders often use these gaps to set profit targets, by measuring the initial move and projecting it forward. Runaway gaps can bolster your confidence in staying with a prevailing trend, giving you the mental fortitude to ride out minor pullbacks and noise.

Exhaustion gaps, on the other hand, appear towards the end of a significant trend. These gaps suggest the final push, where late entrants, typically less informed traders, jump in, driving the price to extreme levels before it reverses. Recognizing an exhaustion gap can be a game changer, signaling that it's time to tighten stops or even consider reversing your position. Unlike breakaway or runaway gaps, which suggest strength and continuity, exhaustion gaps hint at fragility and an impending reversal.

Common gaps typically occur during periods of consolidation or in thinly traded stocks and are usually less meaningful. They tend to be unnoticed gaps that are quickly filled as the market finds its equilibrium. While these gaps are not irrelevant, they require a careful study of accompanying indicators and should not be acted upon in isolation.

Understanding these gaps and their implications can provide traders with invaluable insight into market dynamics. Beyond recognizing the type of gap, the context in which they appear also matters greatly. For instance, a breakaway gap occurring after a prolonged downtrend followed by a bullish reversal pattern like a hammer or an engulfing pattern significantly strengthens the case for a trend reversal.

The interplay of windows with other candlestick patterns adds layers of complexity and enhances predictive power. For instance, a breakaway gap paired with a bullish formation like three white soldiers can indicate a robust upward momentum. On the contrary, a bearish gap followed by bearish patterns, such as the three black crows, underlines a fortified downtrend.

Moreover, the influence of gaps isn't just confined to individual securities. In the realm of indices or commodities, gaps often appear in response to macroeconomic events or sector-wide developments. Understanding this broader context can equip traders with better decision-making tools. For example, a runaway gap in a key market index might prompt you to look for similar gaps in individual stocks within that index, understanding that herd mentality and parallel movements often dictate market behavior.

Another significant aspect of gaps is their role in psychological reinforcement. For many traders, gaps act as both a signal and a commitment mechanism. Seeing a breakaway gap reinforces belief in the new trend, prompting higher trading volumes and further validating the move. This creates a feedback loop that can propel market prices further in the direction of the gap.

It's also crucial to talk about unfilled gaps. A gap that remains unfilled over a significant period is a strong signal of underlying strength or weakness. For instance, an unfilled breakaway gap on a stock chart can suggest that the price level below the gap has now turned into a strong support zone. Traders often place their stop-loss orders just below this support level, confident that the gap will act as a cushion against downward price movements.

Volume analysis also plays a vital role when interpreting gaps. Higher volume coupled with gaps strengthens the indication, suggesting that institutional investors might be backing the price movement. In contrast, low volume might indicate a lack of commitment, making the gap vulnerable to filling. A comprehensive assessment of volume data at the time of the gap formation can provide further insights into the gap's reliability and robustness.

These gaps also represent moments where liquidity is either abundant or scarce. For simply put, a breakaway gap accompanied by high volume tells you there's plenty of liquidity and investor interest at new price levels. In contrast, a sudden exhaustion gap often indicates that the buying or selling frenzy has dried up, leaving the market stretched and primed for a reversal.

Lastly, mastering the understanding and implications of gaps requires practice and keen observation. It is not enough to recognize the patterns; you need to contextualize them within the broader market environment. Developing this keen sense of market intuition takes time but offers substantial rewards in trading success.

Windows, or gaps, aren't just voids on a chart; they are loaded with market psychology, sentiment, and predictive power. Day traders, technical analysts, and all market participants can harness their potential to anticipate price movements, execute timely entries or exits, and optimize their trading strategies. The gaps offer a window—no pun intended—into the heart of market dynamics, making them an indispensable tool in any trader's arsenal. Understanding their nuance and context unlocks the full potential of candlestick patterns, boosting your potential for trading success.

Tasuki and On-Neck Patterns

When it comes to continuation patterns in candlestick trading, Tasuki and On-Neck patterns serve as noteworthy signals that can shed light on the future direction of price movements. Unlike reversal patterns which signify a potential change in trend, continuation patterns like these indicate that the existing trend—whether bullish or bearish—is likely to persist. Understanding and recognizing these patterns can sharpen your trading acumen and help you make more informed decisions.

Let's start with the **Tasuki pattern**. The Tasuki pattern comes in two forms: Bullish Tasuki and Bearish Tasuki. Identifying these can be quite straightforward once you know what to look for. A Bullish Tasuki is typically observed within an ongoing uptrend. It consists of three candlesticks: the first is a long white (or green) candlestick, followed by a short black (or red) candlestick that gaps up from the first, and the third candlestick is another white one that closes into the gap created by the black candle.

The mechanics behind the Bullish Tasuki revolve around a brief pullback during an uptrend that doesn't hold, pushing the price higher again. It's like a pause where sellers give it a shot, but buyers regain control, creating an excellent opportunity for long positions. This pattern doesn't just showcase market behavior but also implicates that investor confidence remains firm in the ongoing trend.

A **Bearish Tasuki,** on the other hand, appears in a downtrend. Here, the first candlestick is a long black one, followed by a small white candlestick that gaps down. The third candlestick in this formation is another black one which fills the gap made by the white candlestick. This pattern demonstrates a brief interruption in the downtrend, where buyers try to push the price up, but the effort is short-lived, and sellers take control again. It usually signals that the existing downward momentum is poised to continue.

In both types of Tasuki patterns, the key takeaway is that the gap is not filled completely, and the trend resumes, reinforcing the prevailing sentiment. For traders, this serves as an important validation before committing to a trade in the direction of the trend.

Now, let's shift gears to **On-Neck patterns**. The On-Neck pattern is another continuation pattern but is more commonly associated with downtrends. This pattern consists of two consecutive candlesticks. The first is a long black candlestick, signaling a strong selling day. The next candlestick is a white one that opens below the previous day's close and closes barely above the low of the prior black candlestick, creating what seems like 'hanging off' the neck of the first candle.

What's fascinating about the On-Neck pattern is its psychology. When you see this configuration, it represents a tepid buying pressure after a strong selling day. However, the buying is not enough to shift the momentum. Often, On-Neck patterns are viewed as indecisive pauses within a strong bearish trend, providing little relief to bulls.

Understanding the context and the exact formations of these patterns is crucial. For example, if during a strong downtrend, you observe an On-Neck pattern, it signals that sellers are still in control despite a minor attempt by buyers to halt the advance. Hence, market players may choose to hold their short positions or even add to them, expecting the trend to continue downward.

It's not merely about recognizing these patterns but also about understanding the story they tell about market psychology. Both Tasuki and On-Neck patterns encapsulate brief interludes in the broader trend direction. They tell us that interruptions in a prevailing trend don't necessarily signify reversals. Therefore, these momentary pauses can be advantageous entry points for traders looking to trade with the trend rather than against it.

Flowing with the existing trend offers advantages in terms of reduced risk and better alignment with market sentiment. However, it's essential to corroborate these signals with other technical indicators and tools, such as volume analysis or moving averages, to enhance your trading strategy. No pattern exists in isolation, and it's the amalgamation of various indicators that provides a robust framework for making trading decisions.

Incorporating Tasuki and On-Neck patterns into your trading toolkit allows you to capitalize on the prevailing market momentum. When combined with diligent risk management practices, these patterns can significantly improve your trading performance. For example, placing a stop-loss order just below the lowest point in a Bullish Tasuki pattern can protect you from unforeseen reversals while maximizing your potential gains as the trend resumes.

To sum up, both Tasuki and On-Neck patterns serve as insightful continuations in the realm of candlestick analysis. They help you anticipate that an ongoing trend is set to persist. Integrating these patterns into your trading strategy, alongside other technical tools, molds a comprehensive approach to market analysis. This adds layers of confidence to your trading routine, enabling you to navigate the market dynamics more effectively.

In mastering these patterns, focus on not only the visual formations but also the underlying market sentiment they denote. This dual approach fortifies your understanding, making you better equipped to interpret price actions and thereby, make well-informed trading decisions.

Next, we'll explore more complex candlestick formations that delve deeper into market psychology and further refine your technical analysis skills. Stay tuned for the in-depth look into Three White Soldiers and Three Black Crows, which promise to expand your arsenal of candlestick patterns.

Chapter 5:
Complex Candlestick Formations

Welcome to the world of complex candlestick formations, where the art of reading market psychology takes on deeper layers. These formations give traders a nuanced understanding of market momentum and sentiment shifts, often signaling stronger and more reliable potential reversals or continuations. Whether it's the Three White Soldiers and Three Black Crows reflecting persistent trends, or the Rising and Falling Three Methods pointing to gradual yet decisive moves, mastering these patterns can significantly enhance your predictive accuracy. These intricate patterns offer multiple signals and require a solid foundation in candlestick theory and keen observation. They aren't just about recognizing shapes, but about understanding the stories they tell regarding buyer and seller behavior. By delving into these formations, you tap into a more sophisticated level of technical analysis, one that unlocks powerful insights and actionable intelligence for your trading strategies.

The Role of the Three White Soldiers and Three Black Crows

The candlestick patterns known as the Three White Soldiers and Three Black Crows offer traders invaluable insights into potential market reversals. These formations are among the most reliable indicators of strong trends and often signal that a significant shift in market sentiment is underway. A deep understanding of these patterns can empower traders to make educated decisions and stay one step ahead of market movements.

The Three White Soldiers is a bullish reversal pattern that typically appears at the end of a downtrend, signaling the beginning of a bullish phase. It consists of three consecutive long-bodied candlesticks that open within the previous candle's real body and close progressively higher. Each successive candle indicates a steady buying interest and a clear shift from bearish to bullish sentiment. This pattern becomes more compelling when volume increases alongside the price rise, further confirming the strength of the turnaround.

Understanding the nuances of the Three White Soldiers pattern involves recognizing the gradual shift in market psychology. As each new candle forms, it depicts growing confidence among buyers. Traders who spot this pattern early can capitalize on the emerging bullish trend, entering long positions at advantageous points. Moreover, the consistency and strength shown by the successive long bodies reduce the likelihood of a price retracement, adding further weight to the bullish outlook.

The counterpart to the Three White Soldiers pattern is the Three Black Crows, a bearish reversal formation. This pattern occurs at the peak of an uptrend and is constructed of three consecutive long-bodied black candlesticks. Like the Three White Soldiers, each candle opens within the previous day's real body and closes progressively lower. The Three Black Crows indicate increasing selling pressure and a definitive shift from bullish to bearish sentiment.

The Three Black Crows pattern offers a stark warning to traders about an impending downtrend. Each successive black candle reveals escalating pessimism, as sellers dominate the market. By recognizing this pattern early, traders can take preventive actions, such as closing long positions or initiating short positions, to mitigate potential losses.

The Three Black Crows is especially potent when accompanied by rising volume, further validating the bearish signal.

While these patterns are relatively straightforward in their formation, it's essential to consider the broader market context when interpreting them. For instance, both the Three White Soldiers and Three Black Crows are more significant when they occur after extended trends, either bullish or bearish. The longer the preceding trend, the more impactful the reversal signaled by these patterns. This contextual awareness ensures that traders don't act on false signals or premature trends.

An essential aspect of mastering these patterns is recognizing the potential for "pattern failure." In some instances, external factors such as economic data releases or geopolitical events can abruptly influence market direction, leading to the pattern's failure. Traders must be agile and incorporate other technical tools, like trend lines and moving averages, to validate the continuation or reversal of the trend suggested by these patterns.

Additionally, traders should consider the timeframe in which these patterns appear. While the Three White Soldiers and Three Black Crows are potent on daily charts, their significance can shift when viewed on shorter timeframes like hourly or four-hour charts. On these shorter intervals, the patterns might indicate shorter-term trend reversals, providing opportunities for day traders aiming for quick profits. Conversely, on weekly or monthly charts, they signal more prolonged shifts in market sentiment, useful for swing traders and long-term investors.

The psychological aspect underpinning these candlestick formations can't be overstated. Both the Three White Soldiers and the Three Black Crows narrate a story of evolving sentiments—whether it's the growing optimism of a bullish reversal or the increasing pessimism of a bearish downturn. Traders who internalize these narratives gain valuable insights into market psychology, enhancing their ability to anticipate and react to future price movements.

Incorporating these patterns into trading strategies requires discipline and a systematic approach. Setting up alerts or automated trading systems can help in timely identification and execution when these patterns manifest. Moreover, coupling the analysis of the Three White Soldiers and Three Black Crows with risk management strategies, like stop-loss orders, ensures traders are well-protected against unexpected reversals or pattern failures.

Examples in historical price charts can serve as practical exercises to deepen one's understanding of these patterns. By analyzing past occurrences and the market conditions that followed, traders can refine their ability to recognize and act on these patterns in real time. Additionally, backtesting strategies that incorporate these formations can offer insights into their effectiveness and provide confidence in their application.

Another critical aspect is the relationship between these patterns and market volume. High volume accompanying the Three White Soldiers validates the strength of the bullish reversal, while significant volume alongside the Three Black Crows confirms the authenticity of the bearish pullback. Conversely, low volume might suggest a lack of conviction among market participants, indicating that the pattern might not be as reliable.

Ultimately, the Three White Soldiers and Three Black Crows are more than just formations on a chart—they are powerful tools in a trader's arsenal. Combining them with other technical indicators, understanding their psychological implications, and contextualizing them within broader market dynamics can significantly enhance trading performance. In mastering these patterns, traders not only read market movements more effectively but also gain the confidence to act decisively, maximizing their potential for success.

By integrating these sophisticated candlestick formations into your trading toolkit, you not only improve your market forecasting abilities but also promote more robust risk management practices. The knowledge of recognizing these critical points of market sentiment shifts can set you on a path to greater trading success and financial acumen.

Recognizing the Rising and Falling Three Methods

In the intricate world of candlestick patterns, the Rising and Falling Three Methods formations are pivotal indicators of market continuation. Their recognition can significantly enhance your trading strategy by affirming the ongoing trend. These patterns are composed of multiple candlesticks, each playing a crucial role in confirming the direction of the trend, whether upward or downward.

Understanding the Rising Three Methods involves identifying a bullish continuation pattern. This pattern typically starts with a strong white (or green) candlestick, indicating a strong buying session. Following this, three smaller candlesticks appear, usually black (or red), which stay within the range of the first day. These smaller candlesticks suggest a short period of consolidation or minor profit-taking within an overall upward trend. Finally, the pattern concludes with another strong white (or green) candlestick that closes above the close of the first candlestick, confirming the resumption of the uptrend.

The Falling Three Methods is the bearish counterpart to the Rising Three Methods. Here, the initial candlestick is a long black (or red) one, signifying strong selling pressure. This is followed by three smaller white (or green) candlesticks confined within the range of the first day. These smaller candlesticks suggest a temporary rebound within an ongoing downtrend. The pattern culminates with another long black (or red) candlestick closing lower than the initial candlestick's close, reaffirming the downtrend.

To effectively utilize these patterns, it's crucial to consider the broader market context. Trendlines, volume analysis, and other technical indicators can provide valuable confirmation. For instance, if a Rising Three Methods pattern forms in an uptrend confirmed by increasing volume, it strengthens the case for a continuation of the trend. Conversely, in a Falling Three Methods pattern, a confirmation with decreasing volume can add weight to the bearish signal.

Patterns don't exist in a vacuum. The Rising and Falling Three Methods are most reliable when seen in context with other market dynamics. For example, a Rising Three Methods pattern appearing near a support level can provide further confirmation of the trend continuation. Similarly, spotting a Falling Three Methods pattern near a resistance level can solidify the bearish outlook.

When incorporating these patterns into your trading strategy, practice diligent risk management. Use stop-loss orders to protect your trade from unexpected market reversals. Position sizing is equally important, as it allows you to manage your overall portfolio risk. Remember, while the Rising and Falling Three Methods are powerful tools, they are not foolproof. Always combine them with other technical analysis tools for a holistic approach.

Monitoring volume is another key step when confirming the validity of these patterns. In the Rising Three Methods pattern, the initial surge should be accompanied by high volume, indicating strong buyer interest. During the three consolidation days, volume typically diminishes, highlighting the temporary pause in the trend. A significant uptick in volume on the final bullish day signals that buyers have regained control, reinforcing the pattern's validity. Similarly, in the Falling Three Methods pattern, heightened volume on the first bearish day, followed by lower volume during the minor upward correction, and a return of high volume on the final bearish day, confirms the selling momentum.

It's crucial to be aware that these patterns may not work well in thinly traded stocks or assets due to the higher potential for price manipulation and lack of liquidity. Their applicability is most effective in larger, more liquid markets where the volume is substantial enough to reduce the likelihood of false signals.

While the Rising and Falling Three Methods are relatively straightforward to understand, mastering their application requires practice. Backtesting these patterns can be immensely beneficial. By analyzing historical charts, you can see how often these patterns have accurately predicted trend continuations in the security you are trading. This practice builds confidence and hones your ability to recognize these patterns in real-time trading scenarios.

The psychological component cannot be ignored. These patterns reflect the battle between buyers and sellers. The Rising Three Methods show a market where buyers are in control, with intermittent selling pressure temporarily halting the upward momentum before buyers once again overpower sellers. In the Falling Three Methods, the opposite is true. Sellers dominate, with minor buy-side interjections that are eventually overpowered.

Understanding the psychology behind these patterns helps traders anticipate market moves. Recognizing that the three smaller candlesticks in both patterns indicate hesitation or profit-taking within a dominant trend allows traders to act with increased confidence when the initial trend resumes.

In summary, the Rising and Falling Three Methods are essential tools in the arsenal of any trader or investor focused on candlestick analysis. Their ability to confirm trend continuation makes them invaluable for planning entry and exit points in various market conditions. However, their effectiveness grows exponentially when used in concert with a comprehensive analysis, considering volume, trendlines, and broader market context. By integrating these patterns into your trading strategy, and through diligent practice and risk management, you position yourself to make more informed and potentially profitable trading decisions.

Chapter 6:
Combining Candlesticks with Other Technical Tools

In this chapter, we dive into the powerful combination of candlestick patterns with other technical tools, enhancing your market analysis and trading strategies. By integrating candlesticks with trend lines, moving averages, and volume analysis, you'll unlock deeper insights into market behavior and improve your forecasting accuracy. Trend lines provide context to candlestick formations, revealing potential support and resistance levels, while moving averages help confirm trends and generate trade signals. Adding volume analysis further amplifies the predictive power of candlesticks, allowing you to gauge market strength and validate signal reliability. Combining these tools not only reinforces your trading strategy but also provides a robust framework for managing risk and making informed decisions in real-time market scenarios.

Candlestick Patterns and Trend Lines

Candlestick patterns, when used in conjunction with trend lines, can significantly enhance your market analysis and trading decisions. Trend lines act as visual guides on your charts, showing the overall direction of the price movement. They provide context for interpreting candlestick patterns, turning them into more actionable signals. By understanding how to draw and use trend lines alongside candlestick patterns, you can improve the accuracy of your market forecasts and increase your success rate.

Let's start with the basics of trend lines. A trend line is a straight line that connects two or more price points and extends into the future to act as a support or resistance level. An upward trend line connects successive higher lows, while a downward trend line connects successive lower highs. The more times a trend line is tested and holds, the more significant it becomes. Combining these lines with candlestick patterns provides a powerful way to validate potential trades.

It's essential to remember that candlestick patterns on their own might give mixed signals. However, when you see a bullish candlestick pattern forming right at an upward trend line, it adds more validity to the bullish signal. Conversely, a bearish pattern at a downward trend line can serve as a strong indication of a continued downtrend. This alignment between pattern and trend line gives traders higher confidence in the anticipated move.

For example, picture a scenario where a Hammer candlestick pattern appears near an upward trend line. Individually, a Hammer suggests potential reversal, but its strength heightens when it occurs near a support trend line. Here, the trend line provides an additional layer of confirmation, suggesting that the market is respecting that support level and likely to move higher.

The combination of candlestick patterns and horizontal trend lines should not be underestimated either. Horizontal trend lines, or support and resistance levels, mark areas where prices have historically had difficulty passing. When a candlestick pattern aligns with these levels, it indicates substantial buying or selling interest. A Piercing Line pattern forming at a horizontal support level, for instance, signals a strong potential reversal from support.

Trend lines are not static; they evolve with the market. Constantly updating your trend lines to match current price action is crucial for keeping your technical analysis relevant. As new high and low points form, adjust your trend lines to ensure they reflect the current market dynamics. This ongoing adjustment helps in maintaining the accuracy of your predictions.

While trend lines provide a visual framework, it is also vital to consider the angle of these lines. Steeper trend lines often indicate a sharper move and could be less sustainable over the long term. Conversely, gentle slopes tend to be associated with a more gradual, sustained trend. Evaluating the steepness of trend lines alongside candlestick patterns can give you insights into the strength and longevity of the current trend.

Also, don't overlook the significance of trend channels, which incorporate parallel trend lines. Channels can predict the price behavior within a confined range. Candlestick patterns forming at the boundaries of a trend channel offer top-quality signals. A Bullish Engulfing pattern at the lower boundary of an ascending channel does not just suggest potential reversal, but also implies the price might trend up within the channel's confines.

Another vital aspect is identifying false breakouts. The market often exhibits what seems to be a breakout beyond a trend line, only to reverse and trap traders. By waiting for a confirming candlestick pattern after a breakout, such as a close above the resistance line in the case of an upward breakout, you can minimize false breakout traps. Patterns like a Three White Soldiers above a resistance trend line provide strong confirmation of a legit breakout.

Volume analysis further enhances the effectiveness of combining trend lines and candlestick patterns. Volume should ideally support the signals given by your candlestick patterns and trend lines. An increasing volume during a breakout or a high-volume Hammer at a support trend line can significantly strengthen the signal's reliability. As a trader, integrating volume analysis ensures you're not simply seeing what you want to see, but what's genuinely happening in the market.

Remember, every market environment is unique. While equities might smoothly follow your drawn trend lines and candlestick patterns, more volatile markets like cryptocurrencies demand additional caution. Volatile price movements can quickly lead to shifting trend lines, so you'll need to be nimble and adaptive. Regularly revisiting and redrawing your analyses can help you stay ahead of the market.

Practical application of these principles requires dedicated practice. Spend time backtesting your strategies, employing historical data to see how candlestick patterns and trend lines could have improved your past trades. This will not only build your confidence but also enhance your intuition for future trades. Utilizing demo accounts and trading simulators allows practicing without the financial risk, ingraining these techniques into your muscle memory.

Finally, your mindset plays a significant role. Emotional discipline is crucial when trading. The best technical setups combining candlestick patterns and trend lines mean little if fear or greed sways your decisions. Cultivating a balanced mindset and following a well-defined trading plan can stabilize your approach. Trust the patterns and established trend lines you've studied, allowing your strategy to guide your trades rather than emotional reactions.

In conclusion, mastering the interplay between candlestick patterns and trend lines can significantly amplify your trading toolkit. It's not just about spotting patterns; it's about context, confirmation, and continuous practice. This combination provides a holistic analytical approach, making your market predictions more robust and your trades more strategically sound.

Combining Candlesticks with Other Technical Tools

Candlesticks and Moving Averages

When it comes to strengthening your trading strategy, incorporating moving averages with candlestick patterns can be a game-changer. Moving averages (MAs) serve as fundamental indicators that smooth out price data and help you identify the direction of the trend. Combined with the interpretive power of candlestick patterns, they provide a robust framework for making well-informed trading decisions.

First, let's establish what moving averages are. Essentially, a moving average is a calculation used to analyze data points by creating a series of averages of different subsets of the full data set. The two most common types are the Simple Moving Average (SMA) and the Exponential Moving Average (EMA). The SMA is a straightforward average of a security's price over a specific number of periods, while the EMA gives more weight to recent prices, making it more responsive to new information.

The beauty of moving averages lies in their simplicity and their ability to highlight the prevailing trend. But what happens when we introduce candlesticks into the mix? Let's explore how these two elements can be combined effectively.

One way to use candlesticks with moving averages is to look for candlestick patterns at significant points relative to the MA, such as crossovers or touches. For instance, if a bullish candlestick pattern appears just as the price touches the moving average in an upward trend, it can act as a signal for a buy. Conversely, a bearish candlestick pattern at the moving average could signal a selling opportunity.

Moving averages can also serve as dynamic support and resistance levels. Imagine you've identified a moving average that consistently acts as a support for prices. When a bullish candlestick pattern forms at this moving average, it strengthens the support level's credibility and provides a compelling buy signal. On the other hand, if prices are trending downward and a bearish candlestick pattern appears near the moving average, it reinforces the resistance level.

Consider integrating moving averages with your current candlestick strategy by experimenting with different time frames. For example, a 50-day moving average may work differently than a 200-day moving average depending on your trading style. Shorter moving averages are generally more suited to short-term trading strategies, while longer moving averages are better for long-term investments. The key is to find a balance that aligns with your trading goals and risk tolerance.

Furthermore, MAs can be instrumental in confirming trend reversals. For example, if you're anticipating a bullish reversal based on a candlestick pattern like the Hammer, you might look for additional confirmation. One way to do this is to wait until the price moves above a moving average before entering a trade. The converse holds for bearish reversals, where a move below a moving average following a pattern like the Shooting Star can serve as additional validation.

Combining candlesticks with moving averages isn't just about looking for alignments; it's also about understanding the context in which they appear. For instance, in a strong trend, moving averages will often slope sharply up or down, and candlestick patterns that signal trend continuation can be particularly significant. On the other hand, if the trend is weakening and the moving averages start to flatten, it may be a signal to watch for reversal patterns in your candlesticks.

To make the most of this synergy, it's indispensable to backtest your strategies. Historical data analysis can offer valuable insights into how effective your combined candlestick and moving average strategies could be under varying market conditions. Such assessments help in refining your approach, identifying potential pitfalls, and increasing your conviction in your trading decisions.

Setting stop-loss orders becomes much more effective when using these combined signals. Placing your stop loss just below a key moving average when entering based on a bullish candlestick formation can protect you from unexpected market downturns. Similarly, a stop loss above a moving average when trading a bearish pattern can hedge against sudden upward spikes.

Nevertheless, it's crucial to remain disciplined and not let emotions cloud your judgment. Over-reliance on any single indicator or pattern can be risky. Instead, use moving averages and candlesticks as part of a well-rounded toolkit. Look at other indicators like volume, trend lines, and momentum indicators to confirm your analysis.

In conclusion, blending candlestick patterns with moving averages can substantially enhance your market forecasting capabilities. This combination not only provides clearer signals but also helps in making more balanced trading decisions. Given the fluid and dynamic nature of trading, there's always room to adapt and refine these techniques as you gain more experience and encounter different market environments.

Your journey in mastering these tools will involve a lot of trial and error, but the dedication will pay off. The key is to keep learning, stay disciplined, and continually adapt your strategies based on the insights you gain from the market. Trading is not just about making quick profits; it's a continuous process of learning, adapting, and growing as a trader. This amalgamation of moving averages and candlesticks is just one more step toward developing a comprehensive, effective trading strategy.

The Synergy of Candlesticks and Volume Analysis

When you're diving into the synergistic world of candlesticks and volume analysis, you're not just adding another tool to your toolkit. Instead, you're blending two powerful forces that can give you a clearer picture of market dynamics. Understanding how these elements interact can significantly amplify your trading strategies, making your decisions more informed and your predictions more accurate.

Candlesticks, on their own, tell a story of price movements over a set period. They provide invaluable insights into market sentiment and potential future movements. Volume, on the other hand, adds another layer of depth to this story. It represents the number of shares or contracts traded during a specific time frame, acting as a vote count that reveals the strength or weakness of a given price movement.

When you combine candlesticks with volume analysis, you essentially add a polygraph to your market interpretation. For example, if you see a strong bullish candlestick pattern emerge but it's accompanied by low volume, you might question the pattern's reliability. Conversely, a bearish candlestick pattern with high volume might indicate a strong conviction among sellers, making it more likely that the downward trend will continue.

Consider a scenario where you spot a hammer candlestick at the end of a downtrend. This pattern indicates a potential reversal. Now, if this hammer is validated by a spike in volume, it adds weight to the likelihood of a trend reversal. The increased volume suggests a strong buying interest, reinforcing the bullish sentiment implied by the hammer.

Parallel to this, low volume during a forming pattern could be a red flag. Imagine identifying a shooting star pattern which is generally a bearish signal. If the volume during the formation of this pattern is low, the bearish signal may lack the required momentum to push prices down further. High volume would imply that multiple traders agree with the pattern, making the subsequent downward move more probable.

In another instance, engulfing patterns can be either bullish or bearish and convey a strong signal of a market shift. Mixed with volume data, the engulfing pattern's power can be enhanced or diminished. A bullish engulfing pattern on elevated volume after a downtrend can be an exceptionally robust reversal indicator, while low volume could make the same pattern less compelling.

Volume analysis isn't limited to confirming candlestick patterns, though. It's also essential in identifying false breakouts and whipsaws. A breakout supported by high volume is far more reliable than one on low volume, which might indicate a lack of conviction. In trading, false breakout traps are one of the painful experiences a trader can face, and volume proves to be a potent deterrent against such traps.

Consider trend lines and how they benefit from volume analysis. When prices break through a trend line, the volume can tell you whether this breakout is likely to be sustainable. A breakout accompanied by high volume suggests that the trend is supported by strong participation, making it more likely to be enduring. Conversely, a breakout on low volume may indicate that the move is weak, possibly leading to a reversal.

Momentum oscillators, like the Relative Strength Index (RSI) or Moving Average Convergence Divergence (MACD), are often used along with candlestick patterns to confirm signals. Adding volume analysis to this mix can make these confirmations even more reliable. For instance, if the RSI is showing an overbought condition and you observe a bearish candlestick pattern with high volume, the likelihood of a downward correction increases.

Day traders, in particular, might find the combination of candlesticks and volume analysis to be indispensable. The fast-paced nature of day trading requires quick decisions based on reliable information. Seeing a pattern like a Doji, which indicates market indecision, accompanied by a significant drop in volume can help you avoid potential pitfalls. Alternatively, a Doji followed by a strong volume spike in the next session could signal an impending strong move, offering a lucrative trading opportunity.

Volume analysis also assists in distinguishing between healthy and unhealthy trends. An uptrend supported by consistently increasing volume indicates robust buyer interest and the probability of trend continuation. On the flip side, an uptrend on declining volume might signal weakening demand and a potential reversal. This context is vital for traders looking to enter or exit positions, ensuring they don't get caught on the wrong side of a trade.

For positional traders and long-term investors, the marriage of volume data with candlestick patterns helps confirm the longevity and health of market trends. Identifying a bullish pattern with substantial volume at the beginning of an uptrend can be a green light for more extended positions. Conversely, spotting bearish patterns on high volume might alert investors to take protective measures against potential downturns.

The volume also plays a critical role during market consolidation phases. During these periods, prices move within a range, and volume can offer clues about the future breakout direction. If you observe volume increasing on up-days and decreasing on down-days, it might suggest a bullish breakout is more likely. Conversely, higher volume on down-days could indicate accumulation by sellers, potentially leading to a bearish breakout.

With the advent of time and sales data and modern trading platforms, real-time volume information is more accessible than ever. This real-time data enables traders to make more timely and informed decisions, which is critical in fast-moving markets. By watching the volume that moves with candlestick formations minute-by-minute, traders can discern the market's immediate sentiment and act accordingly.

Volume analysis also complements other technical tools like moving averages. When a moving average crossover occurs, the volume can signal the strength of the crossing. A crossover accompanied by substantial volume points to a strong trend formation, whereas low volume might suggest a temporary price movement or noise.

In essence, combining candlesticks with volume analysis equips traders with a near-360-degree view of the market. This holistic approach helps filter out false signals, confirm genuine patterns, and provide a more reliable foundation for making trading decisions. Your toolbox becomes not just heavier but more precise, filled with the right instruments to navigate the intricate terrain of financial markets.

Volume is the force that validates the price action, and when coupled with candlestick patterns, it forms a robust framework for predicting market movements. Whether you're a day trader looking for that next quick trade or a long-term investor planning your next big move, understanding and integrating the synergy of candlesticks and volume analysis into your practice can elevate your trading capabilities to new heights.

Chapter 7:
The Psychology Behind the Patterns

Understanding candlestick patterns goes beyond just recognizing formations on a chart; it's about deciphering the underlying psychology driving market movements. Each pattern reflects collective market emotions, such as fear, greed, optimism, or indecision. When traders recognize a bullish engulfing pattern, for instance, they are not merely observing a sequence of bars but are interpreting a shift in sentiment from selling pressure to buying enthusiasm. This psychological ebb and flow often triggers specific reactions among traders, leading to predictable cycles. Learning to read these patterns is akin to becoming fluent in the language of market sentiment, enabling traders to anticipate moves more accurately and manage their positions more effectively.

Market Sentiments and Candlestick Formations

Understanding market sentiment is crucial for any trader. At its core, market sentiment reflects the prevailing attitude of investors towards a particular financial market. This sentiment is often reflected in the price movements and patterns formed by candlesticks. By interpreting these patterns correctly, traders can gain insights into the emotional and psychological state of market participants, allowing them to make more informed trading decisions.

Candlestick formations are essentially visual representations of market sentiment. For instance, a series of bullish candlesticks indicates optimism and buying pressure, whereas a succession of bearish candlesticks reflects pessimism and selling pressure. These patterns do not just represent random movements; they are the collective result of decisions made by millions of traders, each influenced by a complex mix of emotions, news, and technical indicators.

Let's delve into a practical example. When traders spot a "Hammer" formation at the end of a downtrend, it's often seen as a sign of potential reversal. This happens because the long lower shadow suggests that even though sellers pushed the price down, buyers came in with enough strength to push it back up near the open. This tug-of-war showcases the shifting sentiment from bearish to bullish, giving traders a clue about potential market direction.

On the flip side, patterns like the "Shooting Star" often appear at the end of an uptrend. This formation signifies that the market opened near its low, rallied up significantly, but then closed near or at its low, showing that bears have taken control. The sentiment has shifted from greed and confidence to fear and caution, hinting at a potential decline.

Market sentiment isn't formed in a vacuum; numerous factors contribute to it. Economic indicators, geopolitical events, earnings reports, and even rumors can sway sentiment drastically. For traders, it becomes essential to not just recognize these patterns but also understand the underlying reasons for these movements. This contextual understanding can significantly enhance the accuracy of their predictions.

Another crucial aspect to consider is the volume accompanying these candlestick patterns. High trading volume during the formation of a particular candlestick pattern suggests that the sentiment shift is backed by substantial market participation. Conversely, if a pattern forms on low volume, it might indicate a weaker sentiment shift, warranting caution.

The emotional triggers behind these formations can often be traced back to basic human instincts: fear and greed. When prices are rising, the fear of missing out can drive even conservative traders to buy in, contributing to bullish sentiment. Conversely, in a falling market, the fear of further losses may prompt traders to sell off, exacerbating bearish sentiment. Recognizing these emotional triggers in candlestick formations can offer an edge in anticipating market moves.

For instance, multi-bar patterns like the "Engulfing Pattern" combine several candlesticks to provide a clearer picture of sentiment change. In a Bullish Engulfing pattern, the second candle completely engulfs the body of the first, signaling a powerful shift from bearish to bullish sentiment. Conversely, a Bearish Engulfing pattern displays the takeover of bullish sentiment by bearish forces, hinting at a potential downturn.

While it's crucial to acknowledge these visible signs on the charts, traders must also cultivate a broader perspective by considering other technical tools. Combining candlestick patterns with indicators such as moving averages or trendlines can validate sentiment shifts and reduce the risk of false signals. For example, spotting a Bullish Harami near a strong support level reinforced by a rising moving average can significantly boost the pattern's reliability.

The real magic of candlestick trading happens when traders internalize these formations and develop an intuition for market sentiment. Pattern recognition should become second nature, allowing one to make swift, confident decisions in the heat of trading. This intuitive grasp of market psychology sets expert traders apart from beginners, as it's the subtle nuances and the context that often make all the difference.

However, it's vital to remember that no single method or pattern can guarantee success. Trading is inherently probabilistic, and the market can be unpredictable. Developing a robust trading strategy involves not only identifying patterns but also implementing proper risk management techniques to protect your capital.

Examples such as the "Three White Soldiers" and "Three Black Crows" offer more depth into how market sentiment develops over multiple trading sessions. The "Three White Soldiers" formation is a clear sign of consistent buying pressure and strong bullish sentiment. Conversely, the "Three Black Crows" pattern represents sustained selling pressure and heightened bearish sentiment. Both patterns provide valuable insights into the longer-term mood of the market.

It's instrumental for traders to continuously educate themselves and adapt to changing market conditions. The market is a living entity, constantly evolving and adapting to new realities. Historical patterns and behaviors can repeat, but they can also transform, forcing traders to remain vigilant and flexible.

To sum up, market sentiments and candlestick formations are two sides of the same coin. Mastering the interpretation of these patterns offers a solid foundation for understanding market psychology. By integrating these insights into a comprehensive trading strategy, one can not only enhance profitability but also navigate the financial markets with greater confidence and precision.

Emotional Triggers in Candlestick Interpretation

Understanding emotional triggers in candlestick interpretation is pivotal to mastering the art of trading. As traders, we must realize that candlestick patterns are not just a series of colors and shapes on a chart but reflect the collective psychology of market participants. Human emotions—fear, greed, hope, and despair—play out vividly in the trading arena and are encapsulated within each candlestick.

One of the first things to grasp is that different candlestick patterns evoke different emotional responses. Take, for example, the Doji candlestick. When traders observe a Doji, which indicates indecision in the market, they might feel uncertainty and hesitation. This emotional state can lead to more cautious trading strategies, perhaps opting to wait for further confirmation before making a decisive move.

Conversely, consider the Bullish Engulfing pattern. When traders spot a bullish engulfing candle, it often generates excitement and optimism. This pattern, which signals a potential reversal from a downtrend to an uptrend, can stir feelings of hope and greed. Traders may feel an adrenaline rush as they anticipate a profitable opportunity and might act more aggressively, increasing their position sizes.

It's not just individual patterns that stimulate emotions, but also the context in which they appear. A Hammer candlestick appearing at the end of a prolonged downtrend might elicit relief and anticipation. Traders could interpret this as a sign of a bottoming out and potential reversal, prompting them to shift from a defensive to a more aggressive trading stance. These emotional shifts can lead to increased market activity and volatility.

Greed and fear are perhaps the most dominant emotions that traders experience. Greed can drive traders to hold onto winning positions for too long, hoping for even greater profits, while fear can cause them to prematurely exit trades or avoid taking risks altogether. Candlestick patterns like the Shooting Star or Bearish Harami often trigger fear, leading to rapid selling as traders seek to cut losses or secure gains before an anticipated downturn.

Emotional reactions to candlestick patterns aren't always rational and can often lead to suboptimal trading decisions. For example, a trader might panic when they see a Bearish Engulfing pattern, selling off their entire position without considering other indicators that might suggest the bearish move is temporary. Understanding the emotional triggers associated with these patterns can help traders recognize when their feelings are clouding their judgment.

On the flip side, the Rising Three Methods pattern demonstrates a pause in an uptrend followed by a continuation, often reinforcing traders' confidence in the prevailing trend. This pattern can quell doubts and fears, bolstering a trader's resolve to hold their positions. The emotional trigger here is one of reassurance and reaffirmation in the strategy being employed.

For a balanced emotional response, it is crucial to combine candlestick patterns with other technical tools. By validating patterns with trend lines, moving averages, or volume analysis, traders can keep their emotional reactions in check and make more informed decisions. This multi-faceted approach can serve as an emotional anchor, reducing the likelihood of impulsive, emotionally charged trading actions.

Furthermore, it's vital to develop emotional discipline and resilience. Traders should strive to keep their emotions in check by setting predetermined entry and exit points for trades and adhering strictly to these rules. This discipline can prevent emotional responses from dictating trading decisions. For instance, setting stop-loss orders can mitigate fear-driven moves, while predefined profit-taking strategies can temper greed.

The concept of emotional triggers extends beyond individual trades to the broader market sentiment. During periods of high market volatility, collective emotions can exaggerate price movements. For example, during a market crash, widespread panic can lead to dramatic declines, which are often reflected in the candlestick patterns. Recognizing the broader emotional context of the market can provide traders with valuable insights into the potential sustainability of trends.

In summary, emotional triggers in candlestick interpretation are a fundamental aspect of trading psychology. Understanding how different patterns evoke various emotional responses can help traders manage their own psychological states and those of the wider market.

By combining candlestick analysis with other technical tools, setting strict trading rules, and developing emotional discipline, traders can navigate the complex landscape of trading with greater confidence and effectiveness.

Chapter 8:
Essential Risk Management Strategies

In trading, especially with candlestick patterns, mastering risk management isn't just essential—it's non-negotiable. Successful traders don't just focus on potential gains; they emphasize preserving capital. Implementing strategies like setting stop-loss orders and adhering strictly to them can help mitigate losses when the market moves unexpectedly. Position sizing based on candlestick signals is another crucial element; it ensures that even if things don't go as planned, you're not overexposed. By diversifying these strategies and combining them with a robust understanding of candlestick patterns, traders can navigate the markets with confidence, fostering both resilience and long-term success. Remember, the goal is not to eliminate risk but to manage it effectively for sustainable trading.

Stop-Loss Orders and Candlesticks

Understanding the mechanics of stop-loss orders is crucial for mitigating risks in trading, especially when leveraging candlestick patterns. A stop-loss order is essentially a predefined price level at which a trader exits a trade to prevent further loss. It's a fail-safe mechanism that helps to protect your trading capital, offering a structured way to manage potential downswings.

Integrating stop-loss orders with candlestick analysis isn't just tactical; it's essential. Candlestick patterns provide nuanced insights into market sentiment and potential price movements. By harnessing these insights, traders can place stop-loss orders more intelligently. For instance, if a trader identifies a bearish engulfing pattern, which signals a potential downward trend, they might set a stop-loss slightly above the high of the engulfing candlestick to hedge against unexpected market reversals.

This intersection of candlestick patterns and stop-loss orders isn't about arbitrary decisions. It's about strategic placements. Let's take a closer look at how you can effectively use some common candlestick patterns to set your stop-loss orders.

Consider the hammer candlestick, often seen as a bullish reversal signal. The hammer is marked by a long lower shadow and a small real body at the top of the trading range. When this pattern forms in a downtrend, it heralds a potential shift in market sentiment. In this scenario, a trader would ideally place a stop-loss order a few ticks below the low of the hammer. This ensures that the stop-loss is only triggered if the market truly continues its downward trajectory, offering a buffer against minor fluctuations.

On the flip side, the shooting star is a bearish reversal pattern characterized by a small real body near the low of the day, with a long upper shadow. When this pattern surfaces during an uptrend, it suggests that buyers are losing control, and sellers might soon dominate. Here, a prudent trader would set a stop-loss order just above the high of the shooting star to protect their position if the pattern fails to manifest into a downtrend.

Multi-bar patterns also offer rich opportunities for well-placed stop-loss orders. Take the engulfing pattern, whether bullish or bearish. In a bullish engulfing pattern, where a smaller bearish candle is engulfed by a larger bullish candle, the ideal stop-loss can be positioned a few ticks below the low of the engulfing candle. This leverages the psychological shift from bearish to bullish sentiment while ensuring that your stop-loss is tight enough to prevent significant losses if the market doesn't move as anticipated.

Another technique involves using windows, also referred to as gaps. A gap represents a significant price jump between the closing price of one session and the opening price of the next. Understanding these gaps can aid in setting effective stop-loss orders. For instance, if a bullish gap up occurs, setting a stop-loss order slightly below the gap can protect against the price filling the gap downward, which might indicate a false breakout.

Trend lines are another crucial tool when combined with candlesticks and stop-loss orders. For example, when a bullish candlestick pattern emerges at a support trend line, it offers a confluence of technical indicators. In such cases, placing a stop-loss order just below the trend line can offer a fortified level of protection. Similarly, if a bearish pattern forms near a resistance trend line, placing the stop-loss order just above it provides an additional layer of security.

Always remember, market conditions can change rapidly, and candlestick patterns alone are not infallible. The key is to use them in a broader context, combining them with other technical indicators and sound judgement. For instance, when the market exhibits increased volatility, you might want to widen your stop-loss distance to account for the greater price swings, reducing the likelihood of premature stop-outs.

The use of stop-loss orders should be a dynamic process. Regularly review and adjust your stop-loss levels based on ongoing market analysis and as new candlestick patterns emerge. Trailing stops are particularly useful in this regard. A trailing stop aligns with the price movement, secured by a fixed percentage or amount below or above the market price. This approach helps lock in gains while providing a safety net if the market suddenly reverses.

Incorporate the psychology of trading into your stop-loss strategy. Emotional trading often leads to decision-making flaws. By sticking to predefined stop-loss levels based on candlestick patterns, you reduce the risk of making impulsive decisions driven by hope or fear. Essentially, a well-placed stop-loss order acts as a psychological bulwark against the emotional rollercoaster that trading can sometimes be.

Let's illustrate this with a broader example. Imagine you're analyzing the daily chart of a volatile stock and you notice a bearish harami pattern—a smaller bullish candle within the range of a larger bearish candle. Historical data suggest that this pattern often precedes a downtrend in bearish market conditions. You decide to enter a short position. Where might you place your stop-loss? A logical placement would be just above the high of the bearish candle in the harami pattern. This placement offers both protection and a buffer zone, ensuring that minor market noise doesn't trigger your stop prematurely.

Advanced traders might go a step further by integrating volume analysis. For instance, an increase in volume confirms the validity of a candlestick pattern. Using this volume confirmation in tandem with your stop-loss strategy can further solidify your risk management framework. In periods of high volume, stop-loss orders may be placed closer to the price action, trusting that the volume confirms the pattern's strength. Conversely, in low-volume trading, wider stops might be prudent to account for potential price anomalies.

Lastly, consider the role of technology in enhancing your stop-loss strategy. Many trading platforms offer sophisticated tools and algorithms for setting and adjusting stop-loss orders. Utilize these tools to automate part of your risk management process. Features like conditional orders, which trigger a stop-loss based on multiple criteria rather than just price, can offer nuanced control over your trades. Also, some platforms offer real-time analytics and alerts, providing you with timely updates on market conditions and helping you make informed decisions about adjusting your stop-loss strategy.

In summary, stop-loss orders are indispensable in the realm of trading, and when intelligently aligned with candlestick analysis, they provide a robust defense against market uncertainties. By understanding the interplay between candlestick patterns and strategic stop-loss placements, you arm yourself with the tools to navigate the volatile waters of trading with greater confidence and security. Meticulous risk management nurtures discipline, guards your capital, and ultimately, empowers your trading journey.

Candlestick Patterns for Position Sizing

Understanding candlestick patterns is a fundamental skill for any trader, but leveraging these patterns for effective position sizing can set you apart as a truly skilled market participant. The goal here isn't just to decode what each candlestick is telling you about market sentiment but to integrate this vital information into a rigorous risk management strategy. By doing so, you can not only mitigate potential losses but also optimize your gains.

Position sizing is one of the most crucial aspects of risk management. It's the process of determining the number of units or shares to buy or sell in a given trade. While numerous factors influence position sizing, including account size, risk tolerance, and volatility, understanding how specific candlestick patterns contribute to these decisions can add a rich layer of precision to your trading practice.

Let's start by discussing how different candlestick patterns influence position sizing decisions. For instance, single candlestick patterns, such as the Doji or the Hammer, can be great indicators of potential market reversals, but they should be approached with a certain level of caution. A Doji, for example, often signals indecision in the market. If a Doji appears after a prolonged trend, it could be indicating a potential reversal. In such a case, you might decide to take a smaller position as the market is showing signs of hesitation.

Multi-bar candlestick patterns offer another layer of insight. Patterns like the Bullish Engulfing or the Bearish Harami provide stronger indications than single candlestick patterns. Let's consider the Bullish Engulfing pattern. This pattern occurs when a small red (bearish) candlestick is followed by a large green (bullish) candlestick that completely 'engulfs' the red one. This is a powerful signal that the bulls have taken control, and thus, it could warrant a larger position size. However, it's crucial to also account for other risk factors such as market conditions and your predefined risk threshold.

The concept of blending candlestick patterns with other technical tools is pivotal for accurate position sizing. As we will delve into in Chapter 6, combining candles with trend lines or moving averages can provide more robust trading signals. For instance, if a Bullish Engulfing pattern appears at a support level defined by a trend line, the confluence of signals might justify a larger position size as opposed to relying on the candlestick pattern alone.

Understanding the volume behind the candlesticks is another essential aspect. High volume during the formation of a candlestick pattern often confirms the pattern's reliability. For example, a Hammer pattern with high volume can indicate a strong buying interest turning the market's direction. Thus, you might decide to take a larger position, especially in comparison to a Hammer formed on low volume.

But how much should you really risk? This is where your risk management rules come into play. One commonly used rule is the 2% rule, which suggests you should never risk more than 2% of your trading capital on a single trade. If your trading account is $50,000, the risk of any trade should not exceed $1,000. By understanding the likelihood of success indicated by different candlestick patterns, you can more accurately adjust your position size within this 2% risk framework. For instance, a strongly validated Bullish Engulfing pattern might encourage you to risk closer to the 2% limit, while a single Doji might incline you towards a more conservative 0.5% risk.

Stop-loss orders, discussed in a separate section, are another vital part of the equation. Properly placed stop-loss orders can help you control your position size dynamically. Suppose you've identified a Bearish Harami pattern indicating a potential downturn. By setting a stop-loss at a strategic level based on nearby support or resistance, you can limit your downside risk and determine the most appropriate position size for that specific scenario.

Emotional control and psychological discipline are also pivotal in effective position sizing. As we'll explore in Chapter 7, emotions like fear and greed can distort your judgment, leading to oversized positions and significant losses. Recognizing reliable candlestick patterns will provide the confidence needed to maintain discipline in your position sizing strategy.

Consider also the broader market context and macroeconomic variables. While candlestick patterns provide valuable insights, they shouldn't be viewed in isolation. For instance, during periods of high market volatility, even the most robust candlestick patterns might behave unpredictably. In such scenarios, it may be wise to reduce your position size to account for this increased risk. Conversely, during calmer markets, you might leverage more aggressive position sizing.

Advanced traders often develop tailored risk management strategies by backtesting their chosen candlestick patterns. By scrutinizing historical data, you can determine which patterns have been statistically significant in predicting market movements in specific markets or trading conditions. This empirical evidence can guide your position sizing decisions, helping you to fine-tune your approach for better results. While backtesting is addressed comprehensively in Chapter 10, its role in validating position sizing strategies is indispensable.

Moreover, leveraging modern trading platforms can enhance your execution efficiency. Sophisticated trading software often includes position sizing calculators, which factor in your risk tolerance, volatility, and candlestick pattern insights to recommend optimal position sizes. These tools can save time and minimize human error, allowing you to focus more on pattern recognition and less on manual calculations.

Ultimately, the mastery of position sizing through the informed use of candlestick patterns forms a cornerstone of any robust trading strategy. It's an ongoing exercise of balancing risks and rewards, ensuring that each trade you enter is aligned with your overall trading goals and risk tolerance. As you grow more adept at reading and interpreting candlestick patterns, this precision in position sizing will offer you a powerful edge in the often unpredictable world of trading.

To wrap things up, integrating candlestick patterns into your position sizing strategy isn't merely about maximizing potential profits but about fostering disciplined, data-driven trading habits. By honing this skill, you not only shield yourself from undue risks but also pave the way for consistent, sustainable trading success. As you continue your journey through the subsequent chapters, keep this balance in mind—where meticulous pattern analysis and coherent risk management converge, true trading mastery is born.

Chapter 9:
Practical Applications of
Candlestick Trading

Candlestick trading is far more than just identifying patterns and memorizing formations; it's about applying these insights to real-world scenarios to make informed decisions. In this chapter, we'll dive into practical applications by examining real-world examples and case studies that highlight the effectiveness of candlestick patterns in various market conditions. We'll also discuss how to build a daily trading routine using these patterns, ensuring you're equipped with actionable strategies that can be tailored to your trading style. The aim is to bridge the gap between theory and practice, offering you a robust framework to enhance your trading performance and, ultimately, your profitability.

Real-World Examples and Case Studies

When it comes to applying the theoretical concepts of candlestick trading in the real world, there's no substitute for examination of actual trades. This section will delve into various case studies and examples to showcase the practical applicability of candlestick patterns. The ultimate goal is to offer readers concrete instances of how these patterns can predict market movements and how traders can effectively leverage this knowledge to make informed trading decisions.

Consider the case of Apple Inc. (AAPL) in late 2018. At that time, the stock had been in a prolonged uptrend for several months.

However, in November, traders began to notice a bearish engulfing pattern. This pattern forms when a small green candlestick is engulfed by a larger red candlestick, signaling a potential reversal. Indeed, the subsequent weeks saw a correction, allowing traders to either short the stock or refrain from buying at inflated prices.

Next, let's talk about the cryptocurrency market. Bitcoin (BTC), given its volatility, offers ample opportunities for candlestick pattern recognition. In December 2017, amidst the much-publicized bull run, a "shooting star" pattern appeared on Bitcoin's daily chart. This single candlestick pattern is characterized by a small body and a long upper shadow, indicating that buyers drove prices high but could not sustain those levels. Following this appearance, Bitcoin's price dramatically dropped, marking the beginning of a bear market. Traders who recognized this pattern were able to exit their positions before the sharp decline.

Another compelling example is from the Forex market, specifically the EUR/USD pair. In March 2020, amidst global uncertainty, this pair showed a piercing pattern—a bullish two-candle reversal pattern. The appearance of this pattern on the four-hour chart signaled an opportunity for traders to go long. Over the following days, EUR/USD experienced a significant uptrend, validating the prediction made by this candlestick formation.

The importance of context cannot be overstated when discussing real-world applications. For instance, let's look at the equity of Tesla Inc. (TSLA) in 2019. The stock displayed a series of three white soldiers, a bullish reversal pattern comprising three consecutive long-bodied candles that close progressively higher. This pattern appeared after a series of bearish trends and low investor confidence. Recognizing this pattern gave traders a clue that the downtrend might be reversing, leading to an uptrend that continued through the year.

These instances highlight that candlestick patterns are not merely theoretical constructs but practical tools that can provide a critical edge in trading. Techniques and patterns discussed in earlier chapters, like the harami and the three black crows, find their true value when we apply them to trades. Let's take the harami pattern as an example. In mid-2021, Amazon's (AMZN) stock demonstrated a bullish harami on its weekly chart. This pattern consists of a large red candle followed by a smaller green candle confined within the previous red candle's range. Following this pattern's appearance, the stock showed a positive trend, rewarding those who interpreted the signals correctly.

Let's not forget the effectiveness of combining candlestick patterns with other technical tools. Consider a 2020 scenario involving the S&P 500 index. The index had shown a rising three methods pattern, a bullish continuation pattern. Traders observed this pattern near a rising trend line, giving additional confirmation that the uptrend would persist. This dual confirmation enabled traders to hold their long positions with greater confidence, leading to profitable outcomes.

To further illustrate the synergy between candlestick patterns and technical indicators, consider the case of Nvidia Corporation (NVDA) in 2021. The stock was in an uptrend, but oscillators like the RSI indicated it was overbought. At this juncture, a bearish engulfing pattern appeared on the daily chart. Coupled with the overbought condition, this was a strong signal to investors that a short-term correction might be imminent. True to form, Nvidia's stock price pulled back, providing an excellent shorting opportunity.

In the commodities market, gold (XAU/USD) is an asset where candlestick patterns often guide trading decisions. In August 2020, amidst economic uncertainty, a hammer pattern—a bullish reversal identified by a small body with a long lower shadow—emerged after a downtrend. The appearance of this pattern on the daily chart was followed by a pronounced rally, underlining the efficacy of candlestick analysis in commodity trading.

Risk management is also crucial, and this is where candlestick patterns can provide additional insights. In January 2021, the Nasdaq Composite exhibited a series of doji patterns—candlesticks that signify indecision. This was a warning signal; placing tight stop-loss orders around these levels would have been prudent. Those who heeded this advice were able to limit their losses when the market eventually broke downward, reinforcing the importance of adopting a disciplined approach.

Beyond equities and commodities, candlestick patterns find relevance in more niche markets like cryptocurrency tokens. Take Ethereum (ETH) in mid-2021, where an evening star pattern appeared—a three-candle pattern indicating a bearish reversal. This pattern was confirmed on large trading volumes, suggesting strong conviction behind the move. Ethereum notably corrected following this formation, validating the bearish signal.

Examining these myriad scenarios, one sees patterns are not merely isolated representations but parts of a larger psychological and technical tapestry. They inform traders about market sentiment, providing a lens through which to interpret the often chaotic nature of trading environments. Importantly, these patterns also serve as educational tools, encouraging traders to study market behavior deeply and make well-informed decisions rooted in historical precedent.

In summary, leveraging real-world examples and case studies is crucial for understanding the practical applications of candlestick trading. Whether it's a bearish engulfing pattern in Apple, a hammer in Gold, or a doji in the Nasdaq, each instance provides learning opportunities that contribute to a trader's growing expertise. Recognizing these patterns in various markets not only fortifies theoretical knowledge but also offers a tangible roadmap for navigating the unpredictable world of trading, ultimately setting traders on a path to better decision-making and increased profitability.

Building a Daily Trading Routine with Candlesticks

Establishing a structured daily trading routine using candlestick patterns isn't just a good practice; it's a necessity for any serious trader. Candlesticks offer a wealth of information about market sentiment and potential price movements, making them invaluable tools for day traders. Let's dive into how you can build a robust routine that leverages these powerful signals.

First and foremost, start with a pre-market analysis session. Before the opening bell rings, spend some time reviewing global market conditions, economic news, and overnight developments. Examine candlestick formations on various time frames to gauge the current market sentiment. This initial screening helps you identify potential trade setups and shapes your trading plan for the day. It's like gathering all your tools before embarking on a project. You're setting the stage for informed and strategic decision-making.

Next, identify your watchlist. Choose a handful of stocks or assets that exhibit the most promising candlestick patterns. This step narrows your focus so you can concentrate on quality over quantity. A watchlist should include assets showing clear patterns such as Doji, Hammer, or Engulfing formations, as identified in the earlier chapters. Keying in on these patterns helps you to target high-probability trades, improving your chances of success. Don't underestimate the power of focus, especially in an environment as dynamic as day trading.

Once your watchlist is set, it's time to determine your entry and exit points. Utilize candlestick patterns in conjunction with other technical tools such as moving averages or trend lines to pinpoint optimal entry points. For instance, a Bullish Engulfing pattern near a significant support level could signal a strong entry opportunity.

Meanwhile, set your exit points using prior resistance levels or candlestick reversal signals like the Shooting Star. Establishing these criteria in advance ensures you have a disciplined approach and avoid making impulsive decisions.

Effective risk management is another critical component of a successful trading routine. Always use stop-loss orders to protect yourself from significant losses. Candlestick patterns can guide you on where to place these stop-loss levels. For example, if you're entering a trade based on a Bullish Harami, place your stop-loss just below the lower wick of the candlestick pattern. This minimizes your risk while allowing room for the trade to develop. Position sizing based on the strength and reliability of the candlestick pattern is another prudent practice. Adjust your position size to align with the risk level of the trade, ensuring you don't overexpose yourself to potential losses.

During the trading day, keep a close eye on intra-day candlestick patterns. Use shorter time frames such as 1-minute or 5-minute charts to observe developing patterns that might offer quick trading opportunities. However, don't lose sight of the bigger picture. Continuously refer back to higher time frames like hourly or daily charts to make sure shorter-term setups align with the broader market trend. This multi-time-frame analysis adds another layer of validation to your trades, aiding in more reliable decision-making.

A crucial but often overlooked aspect of a daily trading routine is journaling your trades. Keep a trading journal where you document each trade, the rationale behind it, the candlestick patterns observed, and the outcome. Over time, this journal becomes an invaluable resource. Reviewing it regularly can provide insights into your trading strategies' effectiveness, highlight recurring mistakes, and help you adapt your approach for better future performance.

Mental preparation is equally important. Enter each trading session with a clear and focused mind. Emotional discipline is essential when dealing with financial markets. Utilize morning routines like meditation or light exercise to set a positive tone for the day. Keeping emotions in check will enable you to stick to your trading plan, execute trades with discipline, and avoid the pitfalls of emotional trading.

As the trading day unfolds, maintain a habit of continuous learning and adaptation. Markets are ever-changing, and so should your strategies. Be open to adjusting your approach based on the real-time market environment. For example, if a particular candlestick pattern isn't yielding the expected results, re-evaluate its context. Perhaps the market volatility is higher, or additional news has come into play. Adjusting your tactics and remaining flexible will keep you ahead of the game.

To sum it up, building a daily trading routine with candlesticks involves a blend of pre-market preparation, focused execution, diligent risk management, and continuous improvement. By adhering to a structured routine, you'll be better equipped to navigate the unpredictable waters of financial markets. Remember, consistency is key. The more disciplined and methodical you are, the more effective your trading will become.

Set your goals, stick to your plan, and continually refine your approach. Mastering the art of candlestick trading isn't an overnight venture but a rewarding journey. With dedication and perseverance, the roadmap laid out here can serve as your cornerstone for building a sustainable and successful trading career.

Let candlesticks be your guiding light, illuminating the path to informed and strategic trading. Now, as you continue to fine-tune your daily routine, remember that every day is a new opportunity to learn, grow, and edge closer to your trading aspirations.

Chapter 10:
Developing a Trading Plan
with Candlestick Strategies

Entering the realm of trading without a well-structured plan can be akin to navigating a city without a map. Chapter 10 focuses on crafting a robust trading plan that leverages the power of candlestick strategies. A solid plan begins with setting clear, attainable goals that align with your financial aspirations and risk tolerance. Incorporating candlestick strategies into your plan involves identifying key patterns that suit your trading style and rigorously backtesting these setups to ensure their efficacy. By thoroughly testing historical market data, you can gauge the reliability of your chosen patterns and refine your strategies accordingly. This chapter guides you through the essential steps of creating a disciplined, informed trading plan that seamlessly integrates candlestick insights, providing you with the confidence to navigate the ever-changing tides of the market.

Setting Goals and Defining Your Trading Plan

When it comes to trading with candlestick strategies, success begins with a well-structured plan. It's critical to understand how to set goals and clearly define your trading plan before diving into candlestick patterns or executing trades. This isn't just about having a roadmap; it's about setting the right expectations, understanding your risk tolerance, and knowing exactly what you're aiming for in the market.

First, let's talk about the importance of setting clear, achievable goals. You wouldn't embark on a road trip without knowing your destination, right? Similarly, in trading, your goals serve as the guiding light that steers you toward profitability. Define what 'success' looks like for you. Is it hitting a certain percentage return annually? Or perhaps it's reaching a specific monetary gain within a set timeframe? Whatever your objectives, they need to be specific, measurable, attainable, relevant, and time-bound (SMART goals).

Goal-setting in trading isn't just about profit margins; it's also about personal growth and skill development. Consider setting goals related to learning new strategies, analyzing past trades, or improving your emotional discipline. These types of objectives can be just as crucial in the long run as your financial targets. Remember, trading is a journey where continuous improvement is key to sustained success.

With goals in place, the next step is to determine your risk tolerance. Each trader has a different comfort level when it comes to risk, and understanding yours is fundamental. Are you comfortable with high-risk, high-reward strategies? Or do you prefer a more conservative approach that minimizes risk but also potentially caps your returns? Assess your financial circumstances, your stress threshold, and your market experience to decide where you fall on this spectrum.

Your risk tolerance will directly impact your trading decisions, including your position sizes and the types of candlestick patterns you choose to trade. High-risk traders might focus on volatile stocks and leverage aggressive strategies like leveraging, while low-risk traders may opt for well-established stocks and utilize conservative tactics like stop-loss orders. Understanding your risk tolerance isn't a one-time activity—it requires revisiting as your financial situation and market conditions evolve.

Next comes the process of defining your trading plan. A robust trading plan incorporates your goals and risk tolerance and lays out the strategies you'll employ to achieve your objectives. Think of it as your trading bible, guiding your actions and keeping emotional decisions in check. Include elements like the specific candlestick patterns you'll trade, the criteria for entering and exiting trades, and the indicators you'll use in combination with candlesticks.

In your plan, detail your strategies for both bull and bear markets. For instance, in bullish markets, you might focus on bullish reversal patterns like the Hammer or the Bullish Engulfing pattern. In bearish markets, you could shift your focus to bearish continuations like the Three Black Crows or the Bearish Harami. This adaptability ensures you're prepared for different market conditions without being reactive.

Risk management is a critical component of your trading plan. Outline your risk management strategies clearly, including the use of stop-loss orders and position sizing based on candlestick formations. This helps limit your downside and protects your capital, which is especially important when market conditions are unfavorable. Setting a maximum loss threshold per trade or per day can prevent catastrophic losses and keep you in the game longer.

In addition to these technical aspects, behavioral rules should feature prominently in your trading plan. Emotions often lead to impulsive decisions that can derail even the most well-thought-out strategies. Develop rules that limit trading during emotionally charged periods, whether it's after a series of losses or even a winning streak. This helps maintain a level-headed approach, ensuring that each trade is based on logic and analysis rather than emotion.

Review and refine your trading plan regularly. Markets evolve, and so should your strategies. New patterns emerge, and old ones may become less effective over time. Regularly assessing and updating your plan ensures that you remain competitive and adaptable. This isn't a set-it-and-forget-it scenario; treat your trading plan as a living document that grows with you.

Also, incorporate a feedback loop—systematically review your trades to understand what worked and what didn't. This could include journaling your trades, noting the patterns, the outcomes, and your emotional state during each trade. Over time, you'll identify recurring mistakes and successful strategies, providing invaluable insights that can refine your trading plan further.

Consider the importance of backtesting your strategies. Before risking real capital, simulate your trades against historical data to gauge their effectiveness. Backtesting can help you understand the strengths and weaknesses of your chosen strategies under different market conditions, offering a preview of potential outcomes. This step can save you from costly mistakes and provide confidence in your trading plan.

Involve yourself in continuous education. The financial markets are not static, and continuous learning is crucial. Attend webinars, read books, participate in trading forums, and consider mentorship from experienced traders. This effort expands your knowledge base, keeping you abreast of new methods and perspectives that can enhance your trading plan.

Finally, remain disciplined. The best trading plan is useless without the discipline to follow it. Discipline in adhering to your plan—not deviating based on whims or unplanned emotional reactions—is what separates successful traders from the rest. Trust in the process you've laid out, even when the market seems unpredictable or when trades don't go your way.

By setting clear goals and meticulously defining your trading plan, you're laying a solid foundation for your trading journey. This discipline and preparation not only improve your chances of success but also make the trading process more systematic and less stressful. Trading isn't just about reading charts and predicting market moves; it's about the diligence, planning, and discipline that drive long-term success. Engage fully in crafting your goals and plan, and let these elements guide you through the complex and rewarding world of candlestick trading.

Backtesting Candlestick Strategies for Efficacy

One of the most critical steps in developing a robust trading plan with candlestick strategies is backtesting. Backtesting involves running your planned trades through historical data to see how they would have performed. This process ensures that your strategies are not just theoretical but have practical, real-world applicability. When it comes to candlestick patterns, backtesting can be a powerful tool to verify the accuracy and reliability of your chosen approaches.

To start with, the accessibility of historical data has never been better. Platforms like MetaTrader, TradingView, and NinjaTrader offer comprehensive historical data libraries and built-in backtesting functionalities. The ease of access to historical data means there are fewer excuses for not backtesting your candlestick strategies. For effective backtesting, it'll benefit you to focus on longer time periods to capture a variety of market conditions and cycles. This will ensure your strategy is versatile and resilient.

Why is backtesting so crucial? Well, patterns that seem profitable in a short span may not perform well in different market conditions. A strategy that works beautifully in a bullish market might fall apart during periods of high volatility or a bear market. Therefore, scrutinizing your candlestick strategies through different phases of the market is not just beneficial but necessary. It's a form of due diligence that separates hopeful speculators from successful traders.

To execute a proper backtest, first, select your candlestick patterns. These could range from single-bar formations like Dojis and Hammers to multi-bar setups like Engulfing and Harami patterns. Once you've identified the patterns you want to test, the next step involves coding these patterns into your backtesting software or employing manual checks against historical charts. The latter, while time-consuming, offers a hands-on approach that can be educational and insightful.

It's crucial to track key performance metrics during your backtesting phase. Metrics like the win-loss ratio, maximum drawdown, and average return per trade offer a quantitative understanding of your strategy's efficacy. A high win-loss ratio with minimal drawdowns indicates a sound strategy, while the opposite calls for revisiting and modifying the approach. Remember that no strategy is foolproof, but understanding its strengths and weaknesses can offer a significant edge.

When you're backtesting, it's important to consider commission fees and slippage, as these factors can substantially impact the net profitability of your strategies. Ignoring these costs can paint an unrealistically rosy picture of your strategy's performance. Use realistic assumptions for commission and slippage rates based on your broker's fee structure and market conditions.

Subjectivity in candlestick pattern interpretation can also be an issue. Different traders might identify or label patterns differently. To mitigate this, develop a clear set of rules for pattern identification. Automated backtesting can help here by ensuring consistency in pattern recognition. Manual backtesting, on the other hand, pushes you to refine your instinct and intuition. Combining both methods often yields the best results.

A significant benefit of backtesting is identifying false signals or patterns that are not as reliable as they appear. For instance, you might find that certain patterns work well only when confirmed by volume analysis or other technical indicators like moving averages. Integrating these insights into your strategy can refine it further, transforming a good strategy into a great one.

It's also worth mentioning that backtesting isn't a one-time activity. The market is dynamic, so your strategies should evolve in response to changing conditions. Regularly revisiting and updating your backtests ensures your trading plan stays relevant and effective. This iterative process helps maintain an adaptive edge, which is crucial in the fast-paced world of trading.

However, backtesting isn't just about numbers and patterns. It also builds confidence. Knowing that your strategies have withstood historical validation infuses a level of confidence that can be a psychological asset during live trading. Confidence mitigates emotional trading mistakes and affirms that your decisions are data-driven and not impulse-based.

Moreover, backtesting is an incredible educational tool. It offers a unique real-world classroom where theoretical knowledge meets practical application. By seeing how different candlestick patterns behaved under various market conditions, you elevate your intuitive grasp of market dynamics. This hands-on learning is irreplaceable and often provides those 'aha' moments that books and lectures simply can't deliver.

Some traders make the mistake of over-optimizing their strategies during backtesting, tweaking parameters to fit historical data perfectly. This is known as "curve fitting" and doesn't necessarily translate into future performance. The goal should be to develop a flexible strategy robust enough to perform well across different conditions, not just optimized for past data.

Implementing the insights gained from backtesting involves integrating these refined strategies into your actual trading plan. This includes setting up alerts, creating checklists, and maybe even adding these strategies into automated trading systems. The seamless transition from backtested strategy to live trading execution marks the culmination of your preparation and due diligence.

All in all, backtesting candlestick strategies isn't just a step in the process—it's a foundational element that reinforces the reliability and efficacy of your trading plan. It arms you with empirical data, enhances your confidence, and ensures you are not walking into the market blind. By dedicating time and attention to backtesting, you set yourself up for a trading career rooted in resilience, adaptability, and long-term success.

As you progress in your journey of building a trading plan with candlestick strategies, never underestimate the power of consistent backtesting. The lessons you learn from historical data and real-world scenarios not only validate your strategies but also refine your trading acumen, transforming you from an average trader into a market-savvy expert.

Chapter 11:
Candlestick Trading For
Different Markets

Candlestick trading isn't confined to just one market; it's a versatile tool applicable across equities, forex, commodities, and the rapidly evolving cryptocurrency markets. Each market has its unique characteristics, yet the core principles of candlestick patterns remain consistent, providing traders with a reliable framework for analysis and decision-making. When trading equities, patterns like the bullish engulfing or doji can reveal potential turns in market sentiment, while in forex, the speed and volatility necessitate a sharper focus on intraday and minor time-frame patterns. Commodities often respond to broader economic indicators, thus intertwining candlestick analysis with fundamental factors becomes essential. The cryptocurrency market, with its high volatility and 24/7 trading cycle, demands adaptability and a keen eye, as traditional patterns might require slight adjustments to account for market behavior. Across all these diverse markets, mastering candlestick patterns equips traders with a robust and adaptable strategy, harmonizing the art of pattern recognition with the science of market dynamics.

Candlestick Patterns in Equities

When it comes to trading equities, candlestick patterns serve as an indispensable tool for decoding market movements and making informed decisions. Equities, or stocks, represent ownership in a company and are traded on public exchanges. Unlike other markets, such as forex or commodities, equities are heavily influenced by company-specific news, quarterly earnings, and broad market sentiment. Understanding candlestick patterns in this context can provide traders and investors with a powerful lens through which to view market psychology and potential price action.

Let's begin by exploring why candlestick patterns are so useful in equities trading. Each candlestick represents a specific timeframe—it could be a minute, an hour, or a day— reflecting the open, high, low, and close prices within that period. This way, each candlestick tells a story. When combined into patterns, they offer insights into potential market reversals, continuations, and overall sentiment. Given the speed at which market news can affect stock prices, being able to read candlestick patterns quickly and accurately can be the difference between a profitable trade and a costly mistake.

Even basic single candlestick patterns can provide valuable insights in the equities market. For instance, the **Doji** stands out due to its distinctive appearance—where the opening and closing prices are virtually the same. This pattern often signals indecision among traders, and in the context of a strong trend, it could indicate a possible reversal. On the other hand, patterns like the **Hammer** or **Shooting Star** give traders clues about potential bullish or bearish reversals. These single candlestick patterns can be especially potent when they occur at key support or resistance levels, providing a clear signal that a trend might be coming to an end.

While single candlestick patterns are informative, multi-bar candlestick patterns often carry even greater weight in equities trading. Take the **Engulfing Pattern**, for instance. This pattern consists of two candlesticks, where the second candlestick completely engulfs the body of the first. A bullish engulfing pattern can signal a strong potential reversal to the upside, especially when it appears after a sustained downtrend. Conversely, the bearish engulfing pattern can indicate a bearish reversal. These patterns are particularly useful because they visually represent a significant shift in trader sentiment from one period to the next.

Beyond the individual and multi-bar patterns, understanding complex formations like the **Three White Soldiers** and the **Three Black Crows** can give traders even more nuanced insights. These patterns are made up of three consecutive candlesticks, all pointing in the same direction, and they often indicate strong future movements. The Three White Soldiers pattern, for instance, is typically seen as a very bullish signal that indicates a strong buying momentum over three days. On the flip side, the Three Black Crows pattern can serve as a stark warning that selling pressure is likely to continue.

Equities are susceptible to gaps—or 'windows'—on candlestick charts. These gaps can occur due to after-hours news affecting a stock's price before trading resumes, leading to a noticeable gap between the previous and next day's opening price. Windows in candlestick terminology hold significant implications. For example, an **Upward Gap** is often viewed as a bullish sign if the preceding trend was upward, while a **Downward Gap** might suggest a continuation of a bearish trend. Candlestick patterns like the **Tasuki Gap** can provide further valuable insights, often indicating the likelihood of a continuation in the current trend veiled by the gap.

One of the most beneficial aspects of candlestick patterns in equities is their ability to provide real-time information about the market's psychology. The **Morning Star** and **Evening Star** patterns, for instance, perfectly encapsulate a shift in sentiment. A Morning Star is identified by a long bearish candlestick, followed by a small-bodied candlestick, and a long bullish candlestick. This sequence illustrates a significant shift from selling pressure to buying willingness, offering traders a clear reversal signal. The opposite applies to the Evening Star, highlighting a potential downturn ahead.

Candlestick patterns do not work in isolation. They are most powerful when combined with other technical analysis tools. For example, combining candlestick patterns with moving averages or volume indicators can add layers of confirmation and confidence in trading decisions. If a **Hammer** pattern forms around a key moving average support level while volume spikes, the likelihood of a bullish reversal increases. Similarly, using trend lines alongside candlestick patterns can further validate potential breakouts or breakdowns.

The real-world application of candlestick patterns can't be overstated. By building a daily trading routine around these patterns, traders can develop a disciplined approach to market analysis. Start your day by quickly scanning for key candlestick formations from the previous trading session. Whether it's a **Harami** or a **Piercing Pattern**, identifying these setups early can set the stage for the day's trading decisions. Keep an eye on how these patterns align with other indicators, such as earnings reports or macroeconomic news, to add an additional layer of rigor to your analysis.

Risk management forms the backbone of successful candlestick trading in equities. Use candlestick patterns to set clear stop-loss levels and define your risk-reward ratios. For instance, if trading a bullish engulfing pattern, your stop-loss could be set just below the low of the engulfing candlestick. This method ensures that if the market moves against you, losses are minimized. Conversely, doubling down on positions without a solid candlestick signal and corresponding risk management can lead to significant setbacks.

In conclusion, mastering candlestick patterns in equities opens up a treasure trove of trading opportunities. Whether you're dealing with single candlestick formations like the **Shooting Star**, multi-bar patterns like the **Engulfing**, or complex patterns like the **Three White Soldiers,** the insights you gain can dramatically enhance your trading effectiveness. The goal is not just to recognize these patterns, but to understand the psychology behind them, combine them with other technical tools, and craft a disciplined trading plan that incorporates robust risk management. Start integrating these strategies today and watch how they transform your approach to trading equities.

Candlesticks in Forex and Commodities

Candlestick trading techniques can be effectively applied in various markets, but their application in the Forex and commodities markets warrants special attention. These markets operate around the clock and are often influenced by global events, making them highly volatile and packed with trading opportunities. The key to mastering candlestick trading in these markets lies in understanding the unique characteristics and nuances that set them apart from other financial markets.

In the Forex market, traders buy and sell currencies. This market's liquidity is one of its most appealing features, allowing for quick transactions without significantly affecting the price. However, with this liquidity comes volatility. Candlestick patterns are particularly valuable in Forex trading because they can highlight potential reversals or continuations within these turbulent environments. For instance, a well-timed identification of a bullish engulfing pattern in a currency pair can signal a reversal from a downtrend to an uptrend, providing a vital cue for a buying opportunity.

Commodities, on the other hand, include assets like gold, oil, and agricultural products. These markets are often driven by supply and demand factors that can be seasonal and geopolitical. The visual clarity provided by candlestick patterns can help traders navigate these complexities. Commodity markets often experience sharp price movements based on external events, and recognizing patterns like the hammer or shooting star can offer significant insights into potential price changes.

One cannot overlook the importance of time frames in both Forex and commodity markets. Shorter time frames such as the 5-minute or 15-minute charts are frequently used by day traders looking for quick gains. Candlestick patterns on these charts can provide immediate signals for buying or selling. On the flip side, longer time frames like daily or weekly charts are used by position traders who aim to capitalize on larger market movements. Both approaches require a deep understanding of candlestick formations to make informed decisions.

Moreover, in the Forex market, pairs like EUR/USD, GBP/JPY, and USD/JPY are heavily traded, and each pair has its behavior and characteristics. Candlestick patterns can help unravel these behavioral traits. For example, a doji appearing after a strong trend in a currency pair might signal investor indecision and a potential reversal. Understanding these subtle cues can be the difference between a winning and a losing trade.

Commodities trading often deals with futures contracts, which can be more complex due to the involvement of various expiration dates and lots sizes. Candlestick patterns can simplify this complexity by providing clear entry and exit points. For example, a bearish harami in an oil futures chart might indicate that it's time to exit a long position before prices start to decline. Recognizing such patterns can provide traders with the confidence to act swiftly and decisively.

It's crucial to combine candlestick patterns with other technical indicators to increase their reliability. In the Forex market, combining candlestick analysis with moving averages can provide stronger confirmations. For instance, if a bullish candlestick pattern like a piercing pattern appears above the 50-day moving average, the probability of a sustained upward movement increases. Similarly, in the commodities market, coupling candlestick patterns with volume analysis can offer more insights. A substantial volume on a candlestick reversal pattern could signify a strong market sentiment shift, adding weight to the trade decision.

Understanding market sentiment is vital. Forex markets are heavily influenced by economic indicators such as interest rates, employment numbers, and GDP statistics. Candlestick patterns can often reflect the collective market sentiment following these announcements. For example, if a long-legged doji appears after a major economic release, it could indicate a market in turmoil, trying to digest the new information. Identifying these patterns promptly can help traders stay ahead of the curve.

In commodities, geopolitical events can cast a long shadow on market patterns. A sudden spike in crude oil prices due to geopolitical tension can often be foreseen through specific candlestick formations. Recognizing a bullish engulfing or a decisive hammer ahead of actual news can provide an early entry into a profitable trade.

It's also worth noting that while candlestick patterns can be powerful on their own, their efficacy increases when used in conjunction with fundamental analysis. In the Forex market, a thorough understanding of a country's economic health can enhance the interpretation of candlestick patterns. Similarly, in the commodities market, keeping an eye on inventory reports, weather conditions, and crop yields can provide additional layers of insight when reading candlestick charts.

Adapting to the volatility in these markets is also essential. Forex markets can experience rapid movements, and traders must be quick to react. Developing a disciplined approach to placing stop-loss orders based on candlestick patterns can protect against adverse movements. For example, placing a stop-loss just below a hammer when taking a long position in a currency pair can help manage risk effectively.

In commodities, the periods of high volatility often follow key reports or geopolitical events. Recognizing candlestick patterns during these high-volatility periods can lead to significant profit opportunities. For instance, a well-formed evening star pattern in the gold market during geopolitical instability might signal the end of a price surge, providing an ideal exit point for long positions.

Finally, mastering candlestick trading in Forex and commodities requires continuous learning and adaptation. Markets evolve, and so does the interpretation of patterns. Trading journals, regular review of trades, and continuous education can help traders stay sharp. Candlestick patterns have stood the test of time due to their simplicity and effectiveness, but they yield the best results when combined with a comprehensive trading strategy tailored to the unique aspects of the Forex and commodity markets.

By understanding the intricacies of candlestick patterns in the context of Forex and commodities, traders can significantly enhance their market forecasting capabilities. This, in turn, can lead to better trading decisions, improved risk management, and ultimately more consistent trading success. So, dive deep into these versatile markets armed with the knowledge and power of candlestick patterns. The potential is limitless.

Pattern Adaptation for Cryptocurrency Markets

The cryptocurrency market is unlike any other financial market due to its volatility, decentralized nature, and 24/7 operational hours. These unique characteristics necessitate a tailored approach to candlestick trading. Traditional candlestick patterns that have been effectively used in equities and forex markets can also be utilized for trading in cryptocurrency, but adaptations are essential for achieving meaningful results.

The first step in adapting candlestick patterns for cryptocurrency trading is to recognize and internalize the extreme levels of volatility inherent in this market. Volatility here isn't just a regular shift; it's a defining trait that can either make or break a trade within minutes. The quick, sharp price changes mean that patterns like the Hammer, Doji, and Engulfing patterns can manifest much more frequently and might often be exaggerated. Therefore, traders need to remain alert and ready to act more swiftly compared to trading in more traditional markets.

Because cryptocurrencies operate in a decentralized manner, they are subject to fewer regulations than equities or forex markets. This can lead to atypical market behaviors such as extreme price swings and flash crashes. The decentralized nature also invites a disparate collection of traders, from institutional investors to individual day traders, all interacting on the same global stage. This variety in participant profiles amplifies the volatility and unpredictability, making precise pattern recognition and timely action crucial components of a successful trading strategy.

Another crucial aspect of adapting candlestick patterns for cryptocurrency markets is understanding the importance of sentiment analysis. Market sentiment, often driven by news, social media, and influential figures in the crypto space, can significantly impact price movements. Traditional candlestick patterns like the Morning Star or Evening Star can still provide valuable insights, but crypto traders must also account for external sentiment drivers. A sudden tweet from a key influencer can cause a swift market move that a candlestick pattern alone might not fully anticipate.

Incorporating real-time data and machine learning algorithms can enhance the effectiveness of candlestick pattern trading in cryptocurrency markets. With the right tools, traders can backtest various candlestick patterns against historical data to identify which setups work best under different market conditions. These advanced tools can provide predictive analytics that offer a more comprehensive view, helping to distinguish between genuine patterns and false signals.

Leveraging multiple timeframes is another way to adapt traditional candlestick patterns for cryptocurrency markets. Given the rapid price movements, examining patterns on shorter timeframes—such as 15-minute or 30-minute charts—can offer early indicators, while longer timeframes like daily or weekly charts can validate those signals. This multi-timeframe analysis helps in filtering out noise and focuses on genuine patterns that align across different intervals, providing a higher probability of success.

Furthermore, liquidity considerations must be taken into account when trading cryptocurrencies. Different cryptocurrencies possess varying levels of liquidity. Bitcoin and Ethereum usually have higher liquidity compared to smaller altcoins. Liquidity influences the reliability of candlestick patterns. Higher liquidity generally equates to more stable formations, while lower liquidity can result in erratic movements and false patterns. Recognizing this distinction allows traders to select cryptocurrencies that align better with their strategies.

Volume analysis plays a pivotal role in confirming candlestick patterns in the cryptocurrency markets. Higher trading volumes often validate the significance of a pattern. For example, a Bullish Engulfing pattern that occurs with an increase in trade volume suggests stronger buying pressure and a higher likelihood of a sustained upward move. Conversely, if a pattern appears on low volume, it might indicate a lack of conviction, making the pattern less reliable.

Stop-loss strategies also need to be adapted for cryptocurrency markets. Given the faster price swings, placing stop-loss orders too tight can result in premature exits from potentially profitable trades. On the other hand, setting them too wide amplifies risk. Striking a balance by analyzing historical price movements and adjusting stop-loss placements accordingly is crucial. Dynamic stop-loss techniques, where stops are adjusted based on real-time data and price action, can offer a more adaptive approach to risk management.

Additionally, trend reversals and continuation patterns must be carefully interpreted. In cryptocurrency markets, patterns can evolve rapidly; a Bullish Reversal pattern might quickly transition into a Bearish Continuation due to an abrupt shift in market sentiment or external events. Examples like the Rising Three Methods or Falling Three Methods offer insights into continuation, and recognizing these can help in identifying whether a trend will persist or falter.

Combining candlestick patterns with other technical analysis tools such as Relative Strength Index (RSI), Moving Averages, and Fibonacci retracement levels enhances their predictive power. For instance, identifying an Overbought condition on the RSI in conjunction with a Bearish Reversal pattern can provide a more convincing argument to sell. This multifaceted approach ensures that trading decisions are based on a more holistic market analysis.

Furthermore, psychological factors can't be ignored. The euphoria during a bull run or panic during a crash is stark in the cryptocurrency markets. Recognizing these emotional triggers can enhance the application of candlestick patterns. For instance, a series of Doji candlesticks might indicate indecision in the market, often leading to a significant move once a clear direction is established. Understanding the psychology behind such indecisiveness can offer traders a competitive edge.

Finally, the global and non-stop nature of cryptocurrency trading means there's no market close, which impacts the formation of certain patterns that are typically seen in traditional markets at open or close hours. Traders must adjust their strategies to accommodate continuous market activity, often using software and automated trading systems to monitor and act on patterns, even during off-hours.

Adapting candlestick patterns for cryptocurrency markets isn't just about recognizing the formations; it's about integrating them with a comprehensive trading strategy that includes real-time sentiment analysis, liquidity considerations, volume verification, and multi-timeframe integration. In doing so, traders can better navigate the tumultuous waters of the cryptocurrency market, striking a balance between opportunity and risk.

Chapter 12:
Mastering Technical Analysis
with Candlesticks

To master technical analysis with candlesticks, traders must integrate these potent visual tools into a comprehensive technical framework. By harnessing the intricate details provided by candlestick formations, alongside other technical indicators such as trend lines, moving averages, and volume data, you can achieve a holistic view of market movements. This chapter dives deep into advanced chart analysis techniques, enabling you to recognize not just isolated patterns but their broader context within market trends. You'll learn how to synthesize these elements, refining your ability to predict future price actions more accurately. Remember, the goal isn't just to identify patterns; it's to understand the market psychology behind them, paving the way for more informed and confident trading decisions.

Integrating Candlesticks into a Broader Technical Analysis Framework

When stepping into the world of technical analysis, it's crucial to recognize that candlestick patterns aren't just solitary tools but vital cogs within a larger mechanism. Integrating candlesticks into a broader technical analysis framework can provide a more complete and nuanced view of market behavior. With each swaying wick and robust body telling a story, candlesticks offer invaluable insights into market trends, potential reversals, and continuation patterns. But to leverage their full potential, it's essential to combine them with other technical tools and principles.

One of the most effective ways to enrich your technical analysis is by pairing candlestick patterns with trend lines. Trend lines, which connect significant highs or lows, serve as visual representations of support and resistance levels. When a powerful candlestick pattern, like a hammer or shooting star, appears in proximity to these lines, it can provide a more reliable confirmation of potential market movements. For instance, a bullish engulfing pattern near a rising trend line may significantly bolster the probability of a bullish trend continuation.

Moving averages also play a pivotal role when integrated with candlestick analysis. They smooth out price data over a specified period, giving traders a clearer view of the overall trend. When candlesticks align with moving averages, they can offer compelling signals. A golden cross, where a short-term moving average crosses above a long-term moving average, combined with a bullish candlestick pattern, like three white soldiers, presents a robust buy signal. Conversely, a death cross coupled with bearish candlesticks, such as three black crows, signals a potential downtrend.

Volume analysis is another critical aspect of integrating candlesticks into a holistic technical framework. Volume provides context, showing the strength of a price movement. High trading volume accompanying a significant candlestick pattern can validate the move, while low volume may signal a lack of commitment. For example, a bullish harami pattern followed by increased volume suggests a more credible bullish reversal. On the other hand, a similar pattern on low volume might be viewed with skepticism.

Oscillators and indicators like the Relative Strength Index (RSI) or Moving Average Convergence Divergence (MACD) can further complement candlestick patterns. RSI, showing overbought or oversold conditions, can highlight potential reversal points. If RSI shows an overbought condition and you spot a bearish reversal pattern like a shooting star, it heightens the chances of an impending downward shift. MACD, with its signal lines and histograms, helps in visualizing shifts in momentum. A bullish MACD crossover can provide confirmation for a bullish candlestick pattern, strengthening your analysis.

Additionally, Fibonacci retracement levels can act as potent allies in your technical analysis arsenal. These levels, derived from the Fibonacci sequence, are used to identify potential points of support and resistance. When a meaningful candlestick pattern occurs near these levels, it adds weight to the analysis. Suppose a piercing pattern forms at a 61.8% Fibonacci retracement level; the likelihood of a significant bullish reversal increases, providing a clearer trading signal.

Chart patterns, such as head and shoulders, double tops, and triangles, provide structural insights into market psychology and behavior. Candlesticks within these formations can offer timely entry and exit points. If you're observing an ascending triangle and a breakout is accompanied by a long bullish candlestick, this confluence of signals can dramatically increase the probability of a successful trade. Likewise, during a head and shoulders formation, bearish candlesticks at the neckline weaken the support and affirm the bearish outlook.

Bollinger Bands, which encompass price action within two standard deviations, can work harmoniously with candlestick patterns. When candlesticks touch the upper or lower band, it often signals extreme price conditions. A bearish engulfing pattern forming at the upper Bollinger Band implies a strong potential for downside correction, while a bullish pattern at the lower band indicates upside potential. These scenarios can help traders anticipate and react to the market's ebb and flow more effectively.

Market sentiment indicators, often overlooked, can add another layer to your analysis, providing insight into the general mood of the market participants. When the overall sentiment is analyzed alongside candlestick patterns, it helps in understanding the broader context. For example, if market sentiment indicators suggest extreme pessimism and you observe a morning star pattern, it could be an opportune moment to consider contrarian trading strategies.

When integrating candlesticks into your broader technical analysis toolkit, it's also essential to consider the time frames you are analyzing. Shorter time frames can offer more signals but often come with higher noise, whereas longer time frames might deliver more reliable patterns. Cross-validation across multiple time frames can lead to more accurate and reliable trading decisions. For instance, a daily chart showing a bullish engulfing pattern, while the weekly chart reveals a golden cross, presents a very strong bullish signal.

Risk management principles, often neglected in pure technical analysis discussions, are crucial when relying on candlesticks. Candlestick patterns should inform your stop-loss placements, helping to minimize potential losses. By aligning your stop-loss levels with key candlestick patterns, you gain an additional layer of security. For instance, setting a stop-loss just below the low of a hammer pattern can be an effective strategy, limiting downside risk while allowing for potential gains.

Psychological aspects play an unignorable role in integrating candlesticks within a broader context. Traders' emotions, fears, and hopes are often encapsulated in the candlesticks they form. Understanding the sentiment behind patterns, whether it's panic selling or exuberant buying, helps in making better-informed decisions. This psychological insight, combined with technical indicators, forms a holistic view, considerably enhancing analysis accuracy.

In conclusion, integrating candlesticks into a broader technical analysis framework is not merely an option but a necessity for those seeking comprehensive market insights. By combining candlestick patterns with trend lines, moving averages, volume analysis, oscillators, Fibonacci retracements, chart patterns, Bollinger Bands, and market sentiment indicators, you create a multifaceted approach that offers better accuracy and reliability. By continually refining this integration process and adapting to evolving market conditions, you can master the art of technical analysis with candlesticks, making informed and strategic trading decisions that stand the test of time.

Advanced Chart Analysis Using Candlesticks

The journey into advanced chart analysis with candlesticks begins where the fundamental understanding leaves off. It's the next frontier for those traders and investors who want to elevate their game from merely recognizing patterns to interpreting them within the broader context of market dynamics. Advanced chart analysis is not just about identifying specific candlesticks but understanding what those candlesticks imply about market sentiment, trends, and potential future movements.

Diving into advanced analysis starts with a deep appreciation of context. Candlesticks can't be viewed in isolation; the surrounding price action, historical chart patterns, and prevailing market conditions all play crucial roles. For instance, a bullish engulfing pattern might suggest a potential reversal, but if it appears at an all-time market high, its significance might be tempered by prevailing overbought conditions. Advanced traders must consider multiple timeframes and broader market contexts when analyzing individual candlestick formations.

Combining Candlesticks with Fibonacci Retracements

One powerful technique in advanced chart analysis involves the integration of candlestick patterns with Fibonacci retracement levels. Fibonacci retracements are derived from the Fibonacci sequence and are used to identify potential levels of support and resistance. When a significant candlestick pattern forms near these levels, it can provide a stronger confirmation of future price movement.

For instance, spot a hammer candlestick near a 61.8% Fibonacci retracement level during a downtrend. This alignment could suggest a more robust potential reversal and a higher likelihood of a significant upward move. Integrating these techniques enables traders to make more informed decisions and increase the reliability of their trading signals.

Advanced Volume Analysis with Candlesticks

Volume analysis is another critical component in the toolkit of advanced candlestick chart analysts. Volume considerations can validate the strength and reliability of a candlestick pattern. A pattern formed without substantial volume might be less reliable than one accompanied by high trading volumes.

For instance, consider a bullish engulfing pattern whose formation coincides with a spike in trading volume. This surge in volume indicates a strong buying interest, adding credibility to the pattern and increasing the likelihood of a sustained upward move. Conversely, understanding that low-volume patterns might fail to translate into significant price movement is equally important.

Examining Candlestick Patterns in Multiple Timeframes

Advanced chart analysis also requires the examination of candlestick patterns across multiple timeframes. While a particular pattern might be forming on a daily chart, it's essential to check weekly and monthly charts to corroborate the signal. Higher timeframe congruence often strengthens the validity of a pattern.

Take, for instance, a doji candlestick on a daily chart signaling indecision. Should this same doji be part of a larger bullish setup on a weekly chart, the confidence in its predictive power increases manifold. This multi-timeframe analysis ensures that signals are not viewed in isolation but as part of a more extensive market tapestry.

The Art of Pattern Confluence

Pattern confluence refers to the simultaneous occurrence of multiple technical indicators pointing to the same conclusion. In advanced candlestick analysis, this might mean recognizing a bullish engulfing pattern that coincides with a break above a key moving average and is supported by a favorable RSI (Relative Strength Index) reading.

Such pattern confluence enhances the credibility of the candlestick signal. When multiple independent indicators align, the probability of accurately predicting future price movement increases. This approach embodies the essence of a well-rounded technical analysis strategy, integrating various tools and techniques to form a cohesive view.

Using Candlesticks for Tactical Entry and Exit Points

Advanced traders often utilize candlestick patterns to fine-tune their entry and exit points. By leveraging minute details within the candlestick structures, traders can identify optimal points for entering or exiting positions. For instance, inside bar patterns within broader trends can serve as decisive points for initiating trades, offering low-risk entries.

Likewise, understanding the precise moment to exit a trade based on candlestick formations can be a game-changer. An experienced trader might exit a long position upon spotting a bearish engulfing pattern after a prolonged uptrend, preempting potential market downturns and safeguarding profits.

Interpreting Market Sentiment Through Candlestick Clusters

Another advanced technique involves the interpretation of candlestick clusters rather than isolated patterns. Candlestick clusters are groups of candlesticks that, collectively, tell a compelling story about market sentiment. By analyzing these clusters, traders can discern the underlying market psychology and anticipate future price moves.

For instance, a series of small-bodied candlesticks with long upper shadows within a downtrend might suggest persistent selling pressure and reluctance of buyers at higher prices. Recognizing such clusters helps traders stay ahead of the market sentiment and adjust their strategies accordingly.

Case Study: The Power of Confluence in Action

Consider a scenario where a trader is analyzing the price action of a popular stock. The trader notices a bullish engulfing pattern forming at a critical support level identified through a prior price action and a 50-day moving average. Concurrently, the RSI is emerging from oversold territory, indicating potential upward momentum.

In this case, the confluence of the candlestick pattern with support from technical indicators signals a strong buy opportunity. The trader enters the position, placing a stop-loss just below the support level and targets the next major resistance level. The result? A well-informed trade with a favorable risk-reward ratio.

This case exemplifies how advanced chart analysis transcends mere pattern recognition. It is about synthesizing information from various technical tools, understanding market sentiment, and making actionable trading decisions backed by comprehensive analysis.

Continuously Learning and Adapting

Advanced chart analysis is a continuous learning journey. Markets evolve, and patterns that worked in the past might adapt or change over time. Therefore, traders must remain agile and open to refining their techniques. Staying updated with academic research, market developments, and innovative analytical methods is essential for sustained success.

Moreover, backtesting remains an indispensable part of this process. By consistently evaluating historical data and refining strategies, traders can understand the efficacy of their advanced analysis and make necessary adjustments. This iterative process ensures that their methodology remains relevant and effective in dynamic market environments.

Mastering advanced chart analysis using candlesticks is a quintessential skill for any serious trader or investor. It's about going beyond the obvious, delving into the subtleties, and interpreting market movements with greater depth and precision. With commitment, continuous learning, and the right strategies, anyone can elevate their trading game and achieve their financial goals.

Online Review Request for This Book

We'd love to hear your thoughts and feedback on "Mastering Technical Analysis with Candlesticks"; please take a moment to leave an online review, as your insights help us continue to improve and support fellow traders on their journey.

Conclusion

As you've journeyed through the intricate world of candlestick trading, I hope you've gained a profound appreciation for this time-tested technique. The chapters preceding this conclusion were crafted with the intention of equipping you with both the foundational and advanced understanding necessary to thrive in various market conditions. Whether you're a day trader, a financial professional, or a trading enthusiast, the versatility and predictive power of candlestick patterns can significantly enhance your trading acumen.

The essence of candlestick analysis lies in its simplicity and depth—two qualities that offer extraordinary insight into market sentiment and psychology. From the basic components to complex formations, each candlestick tells a story of market participants' emotions, enabling you to make informed decisions. Recognizing patterns like the Hammer, Doji, or Three Black Crows is not merely about identifying shapes on a chart. It's about understanding the underlying narrative and leveraging that knowledge to forecast future price movements.

Your ability to decode and combine candlestick patterns with other technical tools—such as trend lines, moving averages, and volume analysis—can yield a comprehensive trading strategy. These synergies amplify the predictive power of individual patterns and help you confirm signals, manage risks, and optimize your trading performance. As highlighted, effective risk management, including the tactical use of stop-loss orders and appropriate position sizing, remains paramount. Trading without risk management is akin to navigating a stormy sea without a lifeboat.

Reflecting on the practical applications and real-world examples shared in Chapter 9, consider how you can integrate candlestick patterns into your daily trading routine. Consistent practice, continuous learning, and disciplined execution should guide your trading endeavors. Remember, backtesting your strategies, as advised in Chapter 10, ensures their efficacy and helps you build confidence and competence over time.

Moreover, the adaptability of candlestick patterns across different markets—equities, forex, commodities, and even cryptocurrency—underscores their universal applicability. Each market may possess its unique nuances, but the principles remain unchanged. Recognizing this adaptability not only broadens your trading horizons but also facilitates your transition across different financial landscapes.

Your journey doesn't end here. Mastery in candlestick trading, like any other skill, demands continuous refinement and adaptation. The dynamic nature of financial markets necessitates an ever-evolving approach. Stay curious, keep learning, and stay attuned to emerging trends and techniques in technical analysis. Resources listed in the appendices can serve as valuable references to deepen your knowledge and fine-tune your strategies.

As you move forward, embrace the wisdom shared by seasoned traders: stay disciplined, stay humble, and respect the markets. Emotional control, patience, and persistence are your allies. Understand that not every trade will be profitable, but each offers a learning experience that sharpens your skills and hones your instincts. Over time, this disciplined practice can lead to sustained success and financial independence.

The psychology of trading—underscored in Chapter 7—is crucial. Acknowledge the emotional triggers and biases that can cloud your judgment and strive to remain objective. Cultivating a resilient mindset enables you to navigate the inevitable challenges and uncertainties of the trading world.

In conclusion, mastering candlestick patterns is not just about understanding their shapes and forms. It's about developing a holistic approach to trading that encompasses technical acumen, emotional intelligence, and strategic foresight. By integrating the insights and strategies shared in this book, you are well on your way to becoming a proficient and confident trader.

May your trading journey be filled with growth, learning, and success. Thank you for embarking on this enlightening path, and may your charts be ever in your favor.

Comprehensive Glossary of Candlestick Patterns

This glossary provides an in-depth look at various candlestick patterns integral to technical analysis. Understanding these patterns is pivotal for day traders, technical analysts, investors, finance students, and anyone eager to master the art of market forecasting.

Basic Candlestick Patterns

- **Doji:** A session where the open and close are nearly the same, indicating indecision in the market.

- **Hammer:** A bullish reversal pattern that forms after a decline. It has a small body and a long lower shadow.

- **Shooting Star:** A bearish reversal pattern characterized by a small body, a long upper shadow, and little or no lower shadow.

Multi-Bar Candlestick Patterns

- **Engulfing Pattern:** A reversal pattern where a small candle is followed by a larger candle that completely engulfs the previous candle's body.

- **Harami:** A two-bar pattern where a large candle is followed by a smaller candle, completely contained within the previous bar's body.

- **Piercing Pattern:** A bullish reversal pattern where a long black candle is followed by a white candle that opens lower but closes more than halfway above the previous day's close.

Reversal Patterns

- **Morning Star:** A three-bar pattern signaling a bullish reversal, consisting of a long black candle, a small-bodied candle, and a long white candle.

- **Evening Star:** A bearish reversal pattern with the opposite formation of the Morning Star.

- **Three White Soldiers:** A bullish pattern identified by three consecutive long white bodies with small wicks, opening within the previous body's range.

- **Three Black Crows:** A bearish reversal pattern consisting of three consecutive long black bodies with short wicks, opening within the previous body's range.

Continuation Patterns

- **Rising Three Methods:** A bullish continuation pattern where a long white body is followed by three smaller bodies within its range, and a final long white body breaks higher.

- **Falling Three Methods:** A bearish continuation pattern where a long black body is followed by three smaller bodies within its range, and a final long black body breaks lower.

- **Windows (Gaps):** Areas on the chart where no trading occurs, creating a gap in the price. Bullish and bearish gaps can indicate the continuation of a trend.

- **Tasuki Gap:** A continuation pattern where a gap is followed by subsequent trading in the gap's direction, leaving it unfilled.

- **On-Neck Pattern:** A bearish pattern following a sharp decline where a small white body closes slightly above the low of the previous long black body.

Advanced Patterns

- **Abandoned Baby:** A reversal pattern characterized by a gap separated doji, signaling a potential reversal.

- **Three Inside Up:** A bullish reversal pattern consisting of a large black candle, a smaller white candle contained within, and a final white candle closing above the first candle's high.

- **Three Inside Down:** A bearish reversal pattern consisting of a large white candle, a smaller black candle contained within, and a final black candle closing below the first candle's low.

- **Tweezers Top:** A bearish reversal pattern where two candles have similar highs, indicating resistance.

- **Tweezers Bottom:** A bullish reversal pattern where two candles have similar lows, indicating support.

Understanding these patterns requires practice and close observation. Each pattern tells a story about market sentiment and potential future movements, offering valuable insights for making informed trading decisions.

Appendix A:
Recommended Resources for
Candlestick Traders

As you dive deeper into the world of candlestick trading, having the right resources at your fingertips can be a game-changer. Here are some top-notch materials and tools that will elevate your trading game.

Books and Literature

- **Candlestick Charting Explained by Gregory L. Morris** An extensive guide on the principles of candlestick charting.

- **Japanese Candlestick Charting Techniques by Steve Nison** A classic text that offers a comprehensive look into the art of candlestick charting.

- **Technical Analysis of the Financial Markets by John Murphy** Though not solely focused on candlesticks, Murphy's book is invaluable for understanding the broader context of technical analysis.

- **The Candlestick Course by Steve Nison** A hands-on approach to learning how to apply candlestick trading techniques effectively.

Online Courses and Webinars

- **Udemy and Coursera** Both platforms offer a variety of courses on technical analysis and candlestick trading tailored to different experience levels.

- **Investopedia Academy** Courses like "Technical Analysis for Beginners" are excellent for foundational knowledge.

- **Webinars by TradingView** Live webinars that often discuss candlestick patterns and their practical applications.

- **Market Rebellion** Offers several coaching sessions and webinars focusing on technical trading, including candlestick analysis.

Software and Tools

- **TradingView** A powerful charting tool that allows for meticulous candlestick pattern analysis.

- **Thinkorswim (by TD Ameritrade)** An advanced trading platform featuring customizable candlestick charts.

- **MetaTrader 4 & 5** Popular trading platforms that provide robust tools for candlestick pattern recognition.

- **StockCharts** Offers an array of technical analysis tools, including detailed candlestick charting capabilities.

Websites and Blogs

- **Investopedia** A treasure trove of articles explaining different candlestick patterns and their implications.

- **BabyPips** Specializes in forex trading but offers useful insights into candlestick patterns.

- **ChartSchool by StockCharts** Educational content dedicated to trading patterns and technical analysis.

- **Trader's Blog** Hosts articles from experienced traders sharing their insights on candlestick patterns.

Forums and Communities

- **Elite Trader** A forum where traders of all stripes discuss strategies, including those involving candlesticks.

- **Trade2Win** Another active community where you can learn from seasoned traders.

- **Reddit's r/StockMarket and r/Forex** Includes insightful posts and discussions on various candlestick patterns.

- **TradingAcademy Communities** A place to share strategies and learn from community experiences.

Mobile Apps

- **Investing.com App** Provides charts and insights, including real-time candlestick patterns.

- **TradingView Mobile** A mobile extension of the TradingView platform offering full charting capabilities.

- **StockTwits** Connect with other traders and get real-time analysis, including candlestick charts.

- **Yahoo Finance** Offers basic candlestick charting along with financial news and data.

Diving into these resources can significantly refine your trading skills and deepen your understanding of candlestick patterns. Remember, the goal is continuous improvement. As the market evolves, so should your knowledge and strategies.

Appendix B:
Quick Reference Tables for
Candlestick Patterns

For anyone diving into the world of candlestick trading, having a quick reference guide at your fingertips is invaluable. Below, you'll find easy-to-read tables that summarize common candlestick patterns, their classifications, and interpretations. Use these tables to reinforce your understanding and expedite your analysis process.

Single Candlestick Patterns

- **Doji** - Indicates indecision; potential reversal signal.

- **Hammer** - Bullish reversal; found at the bottom of downtrends.

- **Shooting Star** - Bearish reversal; appears at the top of uptrends.

Multi-Bar Candlestick Patterns

- **Bullish Engulfing** - Bullish reversal; large white candle engulfs prior small black candle.

- **Bearish Engulfing** - Bearish reversal; large black candle engulfs prior small white candle.

- **Bullish Harami** - Bullish reversal; small white candle within the prior large black candle.

- **Bearish Harami** - Bearish reversal; small black candle within the prior large white candle.
- **Piercing Pattern** - Bullish reversal; white candle closes above the midpoint of the prior black candle.

Three-Bar and Beyond Patterns

- **Three White Soldiers** - Strong bullish reversal; three consecutive white candles with higher closes.
- **Three Black Crows** - Strong bearish reversal; three consecutive black candles with lower closes.
- **Rising Three Methods** - Bullish continuation; small candles between large white candles.
- **Falling Three Methods** - Bearish continuation; small candles between large black candles.

Gap Patterns

- **Rising Window (Bullish Gap)** - Bullish continuation; gap up between two candles.
- **Falling Window (Bearish Gap)** - Bearish continuation; gap down between two candles.
- **Tasuki Gap (Bullish/Bearish)** - Continuation pattern; confirmation of the gap direction.

Pattern Summaries

To wrap up, here's a quick cheat sheet to help you identify and interpret these patterns on the fly.

1. Reversal Patterns
   - Doji, Hammer, Bullish Engulfing - Potential trend reversals from bearish to bullish.

- Shooting Star, Bearish Engulfing, Bearish Harami - Potential trend reversals from bullish to bearish.

2. Continuation Patterns

- Rising Three Methods, Falling Three Methods - Indications that the current trend will continue.

- Rising/Falling Windows, Tasuki Gaps - Reinforcement of existing trends with gaps acting as support or resistance.

By familiarizing yourself with these patterns and their implications, you can sharpen your trading strategy and make more informed decisions. Remember, mastery comes with practice, so refer back to these tables frequently as you engage with live charts and market scenarios.

www.ingramcontent.com/pod-product-compliance
Lightning Source LLC
Chambersburg PA
CBHW030528210326
41597CB00013B/1067